THE PARACLETE OF CABORCA

That which we do not confront in ourselves
we will meet as fate.

—*C. G. Jung*

THE PARACLETE OF CABORCA

A Collision with Destiny

by

Paco Mitchell

OWL & HERON PRESS

Everett, Washington

OWL & HERON BOOKS

An Imprint of Owl & Heron Press

First published in the United States in 2020

Copyright © 2020

By Paco Mitchell

ISBN978-0-911783-09-4

Text set in Landa

Printed and bound by Kindle Direct

An Amazon Company

Dedication

To The Cow That Died
September 10, 1963
Caborca, Sonora, México

Paco Mitchell

The reality of good and evil consists in things and situations that
just happen to you, that are too big for you, where you are always
facing death. Anything that comes upon me with this intensity I
experience as *numinous*, no matter whether I call it divine or
devilish or just "fate."

—C. G. Jung

ACKNOWLEDGEMENTS

Unless they're churlish, most authors who finish books write acknowledgements, if only because all writers need readers. Thus, a universal sense of gratitude is inevitable, and most writers have recourse to clichés, such as, "I cannot adequately express my gratitude to X, Y and Z." There follows a list of names, perhaps even the name of their cat, sleeping near the clicking keyboard or the scratching pen.

But why such platitudes? I think it's because writers really do feel deep gratitude and indebtedness—and not only to many other persons, living or dead, who helped them in some way, but also to mysterious forces, circumstances and agencies, known or unknown, that not only "helped" them, but proved crucial. Those writers have discovered that the so-called "lonely profession" actually depends on deeper commonalities than they suspected at the start. They thought they were writing!

But how many dead strangers had a hand in forming the language the writers freely use—all the intricacies of grammar, the vocabularies, the poetry? Or prepared the papyrus, the parchment, the clay or the stone? Writers? Some few, perhaps. Just consider: Cuneiform? Hieroglyphics? Hebrew? Latin? Arabic? I capitalize them all out of respect. No wonder writers fall back on platitudes, to offer thanks.

That's how I feel.

Writing The Paraclete of Caborca was a struggle, difficult for many reasons. But at the end, I was overcome by feelings of an almost unfathomable degree of gratitude, flowing in every direction. Unfortunately, a full expression of such gratitude is not possible.

Many friends have helped me over the years—reading versions of the manuscript as it took shape, offering criticisms, advice and encouragement. Every person mentioned in this book, and many others not mentioned—both in the U.S., in

Mexico and elsewhere—are dear to me, and I thank them for all their many kind generosities.

I must also express my singular gratitude to Phil White. Several times throughout this book I wrote, "You saved my life!" Normally, writers seek to avoid redundancy. But without Phil, I wouldn't be here today. How should I calibrate that feeling?

At this point I reach an indebtedness of truly unfathomable depths—the one I owe my parents, Harold and Dorothy Mitchell. The debt is especially evident in the case of my mother, who participated in crucial aspects of the story that follows, calling up the mysteries of life and death, time and eternity.

Now I must acknowledge the efforts of my friend and colleague, Russell Arthur Lockhart. Over many years prior to finalizing this book, with the exceptional steadfastness and gentle understanding of a superb mentor, Russ has stood by me through thick and thin (another platitude that deserves another use). Guiding without demanding, not presuming to know better, Russ never deprived me of the right to make my own mistakes. Why? So I could learn the valuable lessons inherent in those mistakes. In other words, he let me have my own experience. Russ is one of the few "true Jungians" I know—that is to say, he is a "true Lockhartian." Russ's guidance, humor, encouragement and support reveal a profound wisdom. My thanks to him for having the courage to live the wisdom of his own convictions.

No one writes a book alone. You never let me down, Russ.

My thanks to all!

ABOUT THE COVER

THE ASTUTE READER MAY HAVE NOTICED that the *brightest visual element* on the cover of this volume is *the sun itself.* In terms of day-to-day reality that is not always the case, of course, since even the sun can be obscured by passing conditions. But in most *desert* landscapes—as, for example, the Great Desert of Sonora—the sun usually predominates.

Yet for all its photographic brilliance, one cannot say with *absolute certainty* whether the Sonora sun depicted on the cover is rising or setting. It could be going either way—a slender thread of ambiguity I happen to like, since my story depends at crucial points on what is both blindingly bright and blindingly dark.

But just as the sun, with its brightness, dominates the day, so the moon—apart from the artificial illuminations of humans—dominates the night with its subtler, gentler, *phasic* light. The moon forces us to open our eyes wider than usual. And even when it is completely absent, the moon still exerts some degree of invisible pull over our bodies and the watery tides.

Most modern astronomers are not given to poetic effusions, so they tend not to see the interplay of sun and moon—as witnessed from the point of view of Earth—in romantic or mythological terms: an alchemical couple, for example, or the two lovers, or the sacred wedding, and so forth.

With scientific precision we accrue immense gains in exactitude of knowledge. What may not be so clear, however, is how much we lose in the way of *mythopoeic joy*. So much can come from pursuing one's own variations on human experiences that extend over countless millennia—the wisdom and creativity to be found in dreams, myths, poems, art, stories, metaphors, visions, mysteries and so forth; in other words, the higher and deeper aspects and values of the interior world.

One of the keys to psychological health, especially today, has to do with finding ways to *balance* the exact knowledge and power that come from rational thought, with the valuations of finely-differentiated feeling; or to balance perceptive intuitions and insights, with sensate realities; or the outer-directedness of extraverted life, with the veiled qualities of a more introverted life.

When the cultural dominants of the time are overwhelmingly extraverted and "solar," symbolically speaking, then balance will most likely come from greater emphasis on the "lunar" side of life. Many of us have yet to learn just what that implies.

I am not advancing favoritism, by the way—moon over sun, or sun over moon—so much as I am warning against excessive one-sidedness. We cannot do without the sun or the moon, without their radiant realities, or their symbolic riches.

From a lunar perspective, we might say that the sun depicted on the cover of this book is *setting*—a welcome prospect. But seen through the lens of other experiences also detailed in the pages herein, the sun on the cover is definitely *rising.* But whether setting or rising, both directions reveal aspects of what I am calling "mythopoeic joy."

FOREWORD

PAST MIDNIGHT. SUMMERTIME. Tooling along a moonless Highway 2 somewhere east of Caborca, Mexico. Two college guys on a lark before classes begin at Stanford. Carefree. Until that fateful moment. An accident that changed the lives of these guys, and most particularly, the life of Paco Mitchell. In these pages, fifty-six years later, Paco unfolds the compelling story of his near loss of life and the loss of....I will let him tell you that excruciating story.

What I will tell you, is that I have never seen such a clear narrative of fate and destiny both in terms of the prehistory and post history of the unforeseen event. The event itself can only be considered life-changing in major degree. What it opened and produced in the years that followed has been a remarkable journey of twists and turns, a journey still unfolding and most recently giving birth to this singular book.

In trying to understand a fateful event, it is natural to look back, to see if one can discern the threads that spun this encounter on the highway in the dark of night. Paco has spent years traveling the geography of his experiences, his dreams, and compelling synchronicities in search of the prehistory of that fateful moment. What he found was that these earlier events were steppingstones forming a path, as if anticipating, intimating, hinting at "something." What is clear, in Paco's telling, is that fate and destiny may not be singular as we usually think, but plural: destinies and fates. This multiplicity, this complexity, awaits us at every turn, and what we do, what dreams come, what synchronicities befall us, will decide what "is to be." It is clear we do not have a lot of control over these things, yet at each of these points, consciousness in the sense meant by Jung, that is, conscious connection to the depths and not just to ego, can play a crucial role, particularly in terms of the future. In other words, consciousness too, becomes a thread, joining these other threads in weaving the tapestry that becomes the literal story of our life.

Paco's narrative recounts an extraordinary number of synchronicities from early childhood to the time of the accident and beyond that are astonishing. They literally take one's breath away. Synchronistic moments are linked, they have a lineage, a history. They are not singularities happening in a vacuum. One gets the impression from Paco's account, that synchronicities are "alive," or at least produced by something that is alive, purposeful, intentional. I am reminded of something Jung said of creativity, of which synchronicity seems at least a cousin: "We would do well, therefore, to think of the creative process as a living thing implanted in the human psyche." Implanted? By whom? This is the essential mystery.

Paco's awe-inspiring account has the capacity to move the reader in profound ways. You will catch yourself looking over your shoulder and perchance catch a glimpse of this living thing that is at the heart and soul of synchronistic experiences, the deeper dreams, and whatever it is we mean by fate and destiny.

Russell Arthur Lockhart, Ph.D.
Everett, Washington
June 2020

numinous, adj., from Latin *numinosum,* referring to a dynamic agency or effect independent of the conscious will; surpassing comprehension or understanding; mysterious; descriptive of persons, things or situations having a deep emotional resonance, psychologically associated with experiences of the Self.

PROLOGUE

IN 1963, I UNDERWENT A NEAR-DEATH EXPERIENCE that changed my life instantly. Even today, over half a century later, the event still looms in my memory with all the uncanny power of a numinous dream. That near-death experience was the result of a car accident—a common enough event, since they happen all the time. In my case, however, the accident proved to be strange and bizarre.

Years passed before I finally realized that the so-called accident was imbued with meaning, that it amounted to what used to be called an "initiation." Unlike traditional initiations, however, where elders inducted youths into the lore of the tribe or cult in a prescribed manner—often involving forced isolations, harrowing ordeals and symbolic deaths—my initiation was never explained to me. I was never "inducted." It was an *unconscious initiation;* hence, my experience of the event was haphazard, catch-as-catch-can. Yet, I was eventually forced to conclude that everything had proceeded as if somehow ordained.

Compared to the suddenness of the initial blow, the slow process of bringing the reality and meaning of an unconscious initiation into consciousness can at times be treacherous, even dangerous. Such slowness results when one is, as I was, *unschooled* in the ways and means, the values and purposes, of initiation. Our cultural attitudes regarding *what is accidental*—that it happens all the time, that even the origin of life itself was supposedly accidental—versus *what is meaningful*—very rare, and mostly invented or superstitious— these common attitudes had a virtual stranglehold on my ability to evaluate my own experience, hence the long, slow unfolding of gradual realization.

Most of what *was* revealed to me took place over many years in *dreams and synchronistic events,* interspersed with scattered passages read in many books. Thus, I use the term

1

haphazard—so much "chance" was involved. It would be up to me to connect the dots, to find the needles of necessity buried in the haystacks of chance.

Virtually all of the experiences that went into the kettle I tended, as it simmered and cooked for years, were at odds with the teachings of our modern culture. The ingredients that *belonged* were unorthodox, arcane and mysterious. So, rather than plan my life in advance, the way so many of my university classmates were doing, I seemed to stumble from one surprise into another. In fact, I once compared my experience to falling off the upper deck of an ocean liner at night, plunging into the open sea. My classmates steamed ahead on the well-lighted, well-navigated vessel, happily dancing the fox-trot to a live orchestra in the ballroom, sitting at the captain's table sampling vintage wines and so on, while I floundered in the turbulent black waters. Nobody even knew I had gone overboard.

Every day countless numbers of people survive accidents, serious illnesses or near-death experiences far more horrific than mine, and many of those people's experiences might also be considered initiatory. Or they could be, if only they were seen in the right light—seen into, seen through, to what lies on the other side. But too often we ignore the accident's significance or disregard the illness as meaningless, seeing in near-death experiences and accidents—even deaths—*nothing but* the causal, random results of chance "mechanisms," as if we were machines. That's our dominant world- view in a nutshell.

In any event, an inner task has been imposed upon me, to tell the *deep story* of a series of meaningful events that occurred to me or that I witnessed in the course of this past half-century. When I say "deep story," I mean the crucial, synchronistic[1] events that, over decades, marked my periodic encounters with what Jung called *the numinosum*—those stunning, shocking moments when a profound pattern or purpose emerges from out of the welter of experience, and we catch hints and glimpses that point to our deepest character, and perhaps even to our purpose in life.

Some readers may benefit from the hints my story contains, finding encouragement to follow the threads of their own destiny, in the event they too are forced to stray from the beaten path, as I was. Others might find in my story a baleful warning to avoid the treacherous pitfalls of individual experience, and to remain safely contained within the common fold.

A Spanish proverb makes the point poetically:

Ten cuidado, caminante,	Take care, wanderer
De no perder el camino.	Not to lose the path.
Que Dios ha puesto el infierno hell	For God has placed
Muy juntito al paraíso.	Very close to heaven.

4

INTRODUCTION

WHEN THE SUMMER SUN SETS OVER THE GREAT DESERT of Sonora, in Mexico, the heat that accumulates during the day dissipates only slowly, the way it does from an iron ingot snatched from a bed of glowing coals. Here and there across the desert floor, one can see heaving masses of split metallic rocks, so hot they practically bend the air, like powerful magnets. The whole landscape resembles something that was hammered out in a blacksmith's forge.

But despite the forbidding temperatures, vegetation does exist. Most prominent are the giant *saguaro* cacti. Not only do they thrive, but they almost seem to revel in the heat, as if they can't get enough. Across the bleak Sonoran expanse, the saguaros probably number in the thousands. They resemble nothing so much as a stationary army, standing at attention, erect and proud. Their arms are raised in salute to their leader, His Majesty the Sun, who, like a beneficent king rewarding his loyal followers, showers them with gold.

Seen from above, the barren desert resembles an old scrap of parchment, devoid of any text save for scattered punctuation marks—the dots and exclamation marks of shrubs and cacti. The yellowed sheet is torn by sharp gullies, and transected by a straight black line, as if drawn there by a giant hand with a ruler.

That straight line is Highway 2, the main artery connecting Baja California with the rest of Mexico. Highway 2 also serves as an arterial lifeline for the buzzards, the *zopilotes*, that daily soar overhead. For they know that if they are patient enough, Highway 2 will inevitably serve up a feast of blood, and they will live to celebrate another day, another death. Though they generally live off animal carrion—rabbits, snakes, coyotes and sometimes larger animals—they also bear silent witness to a devastating human carnage for which the highway is justly famous. But the *zopilotes* offer no testimony in the court of human ethics, take no position as to the fairness or injustice, the rights or wrongs, of the deaths they observe and from which they often profit. They take what is given and ask for nothing more, although if you try to rob them of their hoard of carrion, they will protest most bitterly. If the buzzards could only read, they might easily discern, from their cruising altitude, the names on the white crosses sprinkled along the roadside like confetti—José Manuel, Ana María, Martín, Francisco, Pedro, Ignacio—the names run on like the directory of an ancient necropolis. For now, the buzzards have retired with the sun, well-fed. But they will be hungry again in the morning and will resume their patient vigil from the sky. Perhaps the highway will prepare their next meal during the night. For, although today was hot, by midnight the air will be a few degrees cooler. Some animals, habituated to the familiar width of the asphalt highway, may doze in its relative comfort; or, if hunting, they might wander across the open roadbed in their quest for food.

But because they all live within the total embrace of a cruel yet generous Nature, who taketh away even as she giveth, they do not stop to think that they might be lining up like sacrificial victims at an Aztec altar, offering up their hearts to the obsidian blade.

PART ONE

South of the Border, Down Mexico Way

GUAYMAS, DECEMBER 1962. TWO COLLEGE BUDDIES, Phil and Mike, and I, decided to travel to Mexico over Christmas vacation. We piled sleeping bags and diving gear into Mike's car, a white '57 Ford hardtop with white-walled tires, and joked our way down to Guaymas, a great adventure for three carefree youths. It was the dry season, the weather was crisp and warm, and we had an exhilarating time. We camped on a deserted beach. The mosquitos did not show up. We snorkeled in the clear, warm water of a remote inlet, and poked around the reefs gawking at sea slugs, starfish and moray eels. We were salty sea-kings of the beach, sunning, swimming, and snoozing like seals.

In town we wandered through the crowds, amazed. I got to try out my high-school Spanish "in the field," and we flirted with the Mexican shop-girls, in the vague hope of getting a date, though God knows what we would have done had they accepted. I was drawn to one girl in particular. Her name was Ramona Figueroa. She was pretty and demure, and I fell in love with the sound of her name. With no possibility of understanding what I was doing, and full of vague fantasies of requited love so typical of youth, I wrote two or three letters to her, in Spanish, on my return home. She never wrote back.

MAZATLÁN, SEPTEMBER 1963. The next year, in the late summer we decided on impulse to go to Mexico again, one last fling before beginning our senior years. Not missing a beat, we made our hasty preparations. This time only one friend could go, Phil White. We took his black Volkswagen.

After crossing the border at Tijuana, we headed east, listening to *mariachi* music on the radio, the commercials boomed out by deep-voiced announcers verging on mania, flogging some *¡producto estupéndo!* But it was all part of our exotic experience—to be in a foreign culture! —even though there was plenty of Spanish *salsa* on the airwaves in Southern California. But this was different. This was the *real thing.* We had passed the border between Baja and Sonora, leaving the populated areas behind, when the desert began to show more of its geological character. Initially, "geology" took the dramatic form of immense, towering, upright rocks. At one point, the road threaded its way upward between a group of these huge, uplifted monolithic slabs. Then it reached a crest and hit a curve before beginning its gradual descent to the vast, tilted floor of the Great Desert of Sonora. At that point, "geology" took the form of the broad desert, which, ironically, was scarcely more than a scarified drainage plain, crosscut and shredded with arroyos and erosion channels. Though it gave the appearance of a dry, barren waste, the entire plain was a testament to the power and evidence of *water.* A satellite view reveals that all the dry waterways converge on the uppermost coast of the Gulf of California. Desert and water, bonded in scarcity and abundance, like an old married couple.

Back to the totemic rocks.

We hit the crest at speed, practically flew over the top, emerged from the rocky defile and entered the curve, whereupon we nearly ran into three donkeys standing on our side of the roadbed. We braked hard and swerved, lucky not to hit any of them. The incident gave us an adrenaline rush, to be sure. We had never seen large animals on any road before, and were not really prepared for *donkeys*—or were they *mules*?—despite the occasional yellow warning road signs with the black outline of a steer, and the word, *Ganados,* "Cattle."

We stopped briefly, got out and looked around at the strange, curiously isolated landscape of red earth dotted with shrubs and small trees. The area seemed to be inside a crater or a bowl. The sounds of our voices reverberated. We shouted a few times, to see if we could hear our voices echoing. They echoed back to us. The animals we had nearly run into, disturbed from their somnolence by our screeching arrival, had wandered off into the scant vegetation. Taking advantage of the interruption, we relieved ourselves behind some bushes, drank some cold bottled water from our ice chest, and soon resumed driving, accelerating through the gears. Pedal to the metal.

There were so many buzzards in the skies of Sonora that I could easily imagine one of them soaring overhead on those huge wings that resembled skysails, watching us from above as we crested the hill and barely missed colliding with the donkeys. I imagined briefly that one of those buzzards had been *telepathic* and had developed the *power of speech* and therefore of *thought* and had seen our little "close-call" episode from its viewpoint high above us. I'm sure that the telepathic buzzard I imagined would have been thinking to itself: "Idiots! Slow down!"

One curiosity we hadn't encountered the previous December, was the series of ominous bureaucratic delays at various highway control-stops, most of which were little more than painted white barricades—sawhorses, basically—blocking the road, or at least our inbound half of it. The guards—or whatever they were—always seemed to find certain mysterious "irregularities" in what we were sure was correct paperwork. And after a few suspicious delays—one of them involving a detour *ninety miles* out of the way to get a meaningless rubber stamp for a $10 "fee" from some puzzled bureaucrat—we plunged deeper into Mexico than we ever had before, bound for the coastal town of Mazatlán. The ever-present buzzards, the *zopilotes*—whether soaring overhead or roosting in the trees along the roadside, patiently awaiting the next road-kill—would have afforded us fair warning of the dangers we faced, had we been alert enough.

This being September, the monsoon season was chugging along like a barometric locomotive with a full head of steam. Daytime highs were in the nineties. Relative humidity routinely hit 80% or more. Heavy rainclouds were continually marching eastward across the Pacific toward mainland Mexico, raking over the southern tip of Baja California and crossing the warm, turbid waters of the shallow Sea of Cortez. As they gathered strength for their daily assault on the north-south Sierra Madre mountain range, billowy, water-heavy clouds in the vanguard would close ranks at the lower elevations and advance up the rocky slopes like Union soldiers clambering up Missionary Ridge above Chattanooga.

We knew nothing of these monsoon conditions until we arrived in Mazatlán, well after sundown. In fact, we had never even *heard* of anything called "the Mexican monsoons." Apart from a few black-and-white photographs in our mid-1950s Spanish grammar textbook—*El Camino Real*—our associations with travel to Mexico all had to do with our single, wonderful trip to Guaymas the previous December.

Rolling into Mazatlán for the first time, well after dark, we drove around until we ended up on what looked like a relatively safe side-street, close to the beach, with one open spot to park the VW. We considered ourselves lucky to find that parking space.

Our plan had always been to save money by sleeping on the beach, as we had outside of Guaymas the previous December. So, although it was dark, and we didn't know if it was even legal to sleep on this public beach, we gamely unpacked our gear and spread out the sleeping bags at the north end of the curving city beach of Olas Altas (Tall Waves)—for tonight at least, *because that was the plan*! God forbid we should change the plan. And, to tell the truth, we were too tired to do anything else.

We couldn't really *see* the beach, partly because it was so dark out (thanks to the delay of that 90-mile detour); partly because we couldn't tell where the high-tide mark was because the entire beach was wet, wind-blown and strewn with sea-wrack; and partly because there were floodlights on the street, pointing seaward, illuminating the otherwise dark, invisible beach and water. The only thing those floodlights illuminated was the rolling, white-foam crests on the relentless breakers as they approached the beach in impressive, serried ranks, then as they crashed, surged and foamed up onto the sand. Ironically, the beach was cast into even darker shadow due to the contrast with the floodlights. Basically, we were light-blind, hot, tired and wet. Then the mosquitos, with their unerring homing instinct, began to zero in.

As for soft sleeping comfort, all the sand on the beach was hard-packed because everything was so wet. The mosquitoes *and* their collaborators the sand fleas were converging on us in droves, mounting their version of a combined military assault—a "coalition of the willing," as we might say. They were utterly determined, and probably jubilant, considering the bonanza we must have presented to them. During the course of the night, as we tried valiantly to sleep, a rising tide forced us awake several times as the water repeatedly encroached, and we had to keep dragging our soggy sleeping bags farther and farther inshore.

Mercifully, the first filaments of a dim light finally threaded their way through the morning overcast, and we gave up any further efforts to sleep. Thus, Phil and I, miserable wretches that we had become, hauled ourselves and our gear to a cheap hotel nearby. At least the hotel offered a degree of sanctuary from the storms, which showed no sign of letting up. After breakfast, we were as ready to go as we would ever be.

Onward!

Undeterred by our mounting fatigue, our lack of sleep or a little weather, we quickly changed into swimming trunks in the hotel room, grabbed our beach towels and flip-flops, and ran back outside to have fun on the beach. But we couldn't skin-dive, since the water was too murky, and we couldn't see a thing. We couldn't body-surf, because the waves were too choppy. Nor could we safely swim, since the undertow and crosscurrents really were too treacherous. We were the only ones on the beach.

We spent three days at that little hotel. The beach was a complete bust, so we tried swimming in a small pool in the hotel's atrium, but the water was green. At least there was a potted banana tree, a small potted palm and low-fired earthenware *saltillo* floor tiles. That was exotic.

We went into town and did some perfunctory shopping. I found a guitar maker's shop and bought a hand-made guitar from him. I had recently begun to learn some basic techniques

11

on the guitar, so this was an exciting find. He charged twenty-five dollars for it. I suspect the wood he used, if not outright greenwood, was at least swollen with monsoon humidity. But I was learning. Maybe twenty-five dollars was not too much tuition to pay for a valuable learning experience—*never buy a guitar in tropical Mexico, made during the monsoon season from unseasoned wood.*

By this time, I was loopy with fatigue. So was Phil. After several days with practically no sleep, we felt like we were in one of those sleep-deprivation experiments that psych-department "sleep labs" carry out on college sophomores, to see how long they can go without sleep before going crazy.

One afternoon we were having lunch in a small courtyard café. This was the most pleasant place we'd found in Mazatlán. Tall tropical trees formed a canopy of branches and leaves overhead, casting welcome shadows over the patio below. Surrounded by a colonnade of white-washed walls surmounted by red-tile roofing, the patio was centered on a small, tiled fountain.

Moving among the tables, two waiters attended their customers, serving food, replenishing drinks. Soft conversations drifted on the air—the heat discouraged loud conversations. Guitar music emanated from a small speaker in a dappled corner, the scratchy sound of a lone guitarist forming plaintive chords and melodies on his instrument. The notes were harmonized, but in a minor key.

Around the fountain, paving stones glistened with the water flung off small birds' wings as they bathed in the shallow basin. Splashing and preening by turns, they darted back and forth between the safety of the branches overhead and the thrilling joy of the fountain. In their direct simplicity, they seemed to create a harmony between what is above and what is below, as if their main task were to unite heaven and earth into one rambunctious, chattering whole.

Even within this protected oasis, however, the air was quite warm and humid. But the shade made it seem less so, and the sounds of splashing water and flitting birds diverted the mind from the body's discomfort. Outside was another matter. There, the air was very hot indeed—almost personified, malevolent, as if it could crack bones. The dense black thunderheads continued to pile up on the distant ridges, but the heat had not quite reached the explosive breaking point, where a violent storm might lessen the tension.

Phil and I lingered at one of the tables. The waiter had cleared our plates and was standing under a *portal*, waiting to present the bill. We were trying to decide whether to prolong our vacation a few more days, as planned, or whether to abort the mission and return home. I say, "abort the mission," using military jargon, though we were just college kids. But the hormonal drive which had gotten us this far produced a headlong intensity that may as well have been military. Were we charging into a hail of bullets or taking a vacation? Take your pick.

"What do you think, Phil? Are you having a good time?" I asked. I was wearing a white T-shirt with lime-green Bermuda shorts and a stiff new pair of *huaraches*, leather sandals with soles cut out of used tire treads. Phil was taller by several inches, had a wiry build, and his black hair contrasted with my blond. He wore dark-framed glasses, cut-off jeans, a T-shirt with missing sleeves, and *huaraches*. We both had developed blisters on our feet, thanks to the stiff leather of the *huaraches*.

Keep in mind that the idea had been to get away from our "routines" in Southern California, do something adventurous. We would be starting our final year of college in two weeks and didn't have much spare money. Since we both spoke some Spanish, Mexico was the obvious choice, and far-off Mazatlán seemed to fit the bill nicely—exotic, foreign, tropical Mazatlán. Huge lizards reportedly swam in rivers not far away. Sting rays and moray eels lived in the shallow bays. Buzzards were plentiful. We would be forced to practice our Spanish. We could buy some of those funny *huaraches* we had always wanted.

"Well, it sure is hot. And I'm covered with mosquito bites," replied Phil. "Same here. And I haven't slept well since we got here," I admitted. "Neither have I. Too hot. Too much noise from the other rooms."

The conversation continued in this roundabout way. The truth was that we were both miserable, looking for an excuse to cut the trip short. We were sick of exotic Mazatlán. We had not reckoned with the hard reality of the summer months in coastal Mexico, the brutal power of the Mexican monsoons. What had seemed like a simple escapade, a lark, when we concocted our plan in Southern California, was turning out to be something else entirely. Like the donkeys on the roadbed, the storm clouds pushing up against the mountains might have served as another early warning, had we been paying attention.

"Should we leave in the morning?" I asked. "It's already past noon."

"Well, if we do, then by the time we cross the desert tomorrow it will be *really* hot."

"Hell, let's just go. It's cooler after dark. We can drive until we get tired, then decide whether to cross the desert tonight or tomorrow."

"Okay," said Phil, "let's go." So much for deliberation.

The spark of a decision ignited an explosion of motive force, as if our brains were combustion chambers and our hearts pumped gasoline instead of blood. Sleeping bags, snorkels, water bottles and duffel bags fairly flew into the rear seat of the VW. Scarcely had we checked out of the hotel before we had filled the car with gas, cleared the city limits and forced the straining engine to redline. It did not occur to us that we had no chance of keeping pace with the disappearing sun, but rather were driving into a darkness that would soon overtake us.

Phil drove first. Though exhausted from several days with so little sleep, he felt it his (military) duty to carry the load. Never say die! For hours the little car inched northward, like a black ant crawling over the sinuous lines on a crumpled map. We drove past towns whose names had seemed enticingly exotic on the way down, but now, with darkness approaching, and our fatigue so deep, the names had begun to take on a more ominous tone: Culiacán, Guasave, Huatabampo, Los Mochis, Bacabachi, Río Muerto. It seemed as if the landscape itself, even the names, were closing in on us.

Something like a living darkness swarmed out of the ground, rising and spreading like a bloodstain on cotton. This was no mere privation of light or meteorological *privatio boni*—a theological "privation of good." This was more like a willful occlusion of the means of sight, as when an operatic *bravo,* like Sparafucile in *Rigoletto*, throws a black hood over his victim's head, just before administering the knife.

It must have been from darkness like this that witch doctors and theologians conjured the existence of demons and evil spirits. Had the early Spanish *conquistadores* felt no apprehension at all as nightfall approached, in these latitudes? Or did it just seem to them like a normal, Catholic dusk, filled with choirs, angels and saints?

We stopped for dinner at a small café near Guaymas. We were too tired to care about décor—oilcloth table covers—or even what we were eating—tortillas and beans. I was feeling the onset of a gastric upset, impishly referred to by Mexicans as *turista*—ha! —so I ordered a cup of *sopa de ajo*, hoping the garlic would drive away the evil spirits, as in the Middle Ages.

If you think about it, fatigue is one of Mother Nature's gifts to us. Like a circuit breaker in an electrical panel, it is supposed to prevent a greater, catastrophic breakdown, by breaking us down in smaller doses. It is a gentle warning sign alerting us to counter-productive tendencies that we might not notice otherwise. *"Eat when hungry, sleep when tired,"* goes a Zen saying. So, if you find that you are tired, then by all means rest, says Nature—unless you happen to be chasing a zebra across the Kalahari Desert for your tribe's weekly meal. In that case, you increase your stamina.

Patriarchal psychology, on the other hand, often derides Nature's wisdom as weak, shameful and cowardly. Rest whispers the Mother. Harden your heart and take the next hill, rails the Father, like Patton driving his army toward Berlin.

If Phil and I had only listened to the murmurings of Mother Nature as we walked out of that tiny Mexican café into the sultry night air, we would have given up our assault on the night desert, found a cheap room—even the cramped cab of the Volkswagen would have sufficed—and simply slept. But our training had not been in Nature's wisdom, it had been in football and track where, if you were tired, you didn't stop, you ran all the harder because—according to the coaches' forever-upbeat exhortations—you were "champions." Not realizing we were caught up in a primordial, mythic tangle, we opted for a compromise. Maybe we could satisfy these conflicting demands by satisfying neither side completely. *We'll keep driving,* we decided, *but one of us will sleep. Then, when the driver can't take any more, the sleeper will awaken.*

Satisfy the Mother but satisfy the Father too, even if it kills you. So, I drove while Phil slept.

SANTA ANA, SONORA, MÉXICO. AT AROUND MIDNIGHT—my head tilted back far enough so I could almost shut my eyes, but they would still technically be "open"—I saw dim lights ahead. It was an all-night gas station at the town of Santa Ana, at the intersection of Highway 15 to the north toward Nogales, about seventy miles away, and Highway 2 to the west toward Caborca, also about seventy miles away. From Caborca, Highway 2 ran on across the desert toward Baja California, to Southern California and to home.

I pulled in at the gas station to fill the tank. Phil woke up. The facilities were dirty but neither of us cared. Relief included splashing some water on our faces. We stepped outside and approached the "beetle." The front of the VW was splattered with insects. It looked like a WWII bomber that had just flown through heavy flak. I made a perfunctory effort to scrape some of the bugs off the windshield, then crawled into the passenger's seat, fastened my seat belt, put my head against a pillow, and fell asleep. Within seconds, I plunged into what might have been the deepest sleep of my life.

With the full weight of night upon us, and my being fast asleep, there was little to help Phil break the monotony of Highway 2, which, apart from the occasional jog this way or that, was mostly straight as a freshly-tuned piano wire. All Phil had to do was keep the car pointed dead ahead, stay awake and look out for obstacles.

Scrubby brush flew past the side windows as the headlight beams bounced along the rough roadbed. Head bobbing—stretching and flexing as much as he could to keep his blood circulating—Phil gripped the wheel grimly. There was no radio station within reach of this desolate zone to provide distraction at this hour. Staring at the blurry windscreen before him, as the headlights jiggled over the asphalt road ahead, he blinked, yawned and flexed.

For some reason, I suddenly woke up at one point, looked at the darkness ahead, then shouted, "Phil, look out." Coming out of a heavy slumber, my voice must have sounded like a bullfrog's. Why did I happen to wake up at that precise moment? It was as if I had awakened from a dream *in order to see something moving ahead of us, and to alert him.*

Phil snapped out of his trance and slammed on the brakes. The VW stopped just short of a freight train that was pulling ratty old boxcars over what may have been an unlighted crossing. Maybe there was a bell, red lights and a swinging "wigwag" sign. I don't remember. The shock of surprise and alarm kept me awake only briefly. Soon I fell back into that deep sleep. The train passed. Phil drove on into the night.

Sometime later the VW hit a black cow.

Phil only had a few seconds to decipher what he was seeing—two black cows standing on the unlighted desert roadbed on a moonless night, blocking the highway. He hit the horn, slammed on the brakes and braced for the collision. There was no turning away, because the narrow roadbed was elevated above the tilted desert floor as a precaution against flash floods. The engineered highway cut straight across the desiccated watershed like an insult—*a slap in the face of water.* Nor was there much of a shoulder anywhere in evidence. For the most part, either you stayed on the straight-and-narrow, so to speak, or you rolled.

From eighty-five miles an hour, Phil managed to brake to about fifty-five, when the impact occurred. At that moment I was still sound asleep, so I pitched forward, like a limp rag-doll pivoting from the waist at the seat belt, against the shattering safety-glass of the windshield, just as the massive body of the cow was slamming into it from outside. Human head and bovine body met at the disintegrating plane of the glass, whose main purpose, ironically, is to protect and enable *vision from within.*

17

"Bob, are you all right?"

"My eye! I can't see!"

We had slithered to a stop. The inside of the car was littered with small pieces of safety glass—like sharp popcorn— the headliner was spattered with blood. One headlight still shone, but at a crazy angle to the road. Phil grabbed a towel, soaked it in ice water from the cooler in back and I held the towel against my bleeding face. Then he jumped out of the car, looked at the damage, got back in and re-started the engine.

Thank God the engine was in the rear, so it was undamaged. The metal of the right front fender was so badly torn that the car could only turn *left*. After some maneuvering, Phil got us pointed back in the direction from which we had just come. Once again, we sped off into the darkness, this time back toward Caborca, the small town we had just passed not long before, while I was still asleep. Phil had to find help in the middle of the night, in a hurry. And he had to do it all in Spanish. *¡Socorro!*

TWELVE HOURS LATER—EL HOSPITAL DE CABORCA. One small room with four beds. Curtains drooped over unscreened windows. Flies passed through the openings. The heat was undiminished. This was the only hospital—and the only hospital room—within who-knows-how-many miles? Probably Hermosillo to the east, Sonoyta to the west. I was lying in one of the beds, asleep. Was this sleep? I was unconscious, by any measure.

For all practical purposes, my memory of the past twelve to fourteen hours had been erased, deleted.

Technically, I was awake for some of that time; that is, my body was sitting, standing, moving, resisting, while my   vocal chords were vibrating wildly, forming words in Spanish, *en voz alta*—in a loud voice.

But for twelve or more hours, basically, I was lost and gone. Whatever happened *inside* me that night, inside the "black box," no one can say. We only know what happened to my delirious body, because there were several witnesses. For half a century now, with the best will in the world, all I can remember of that period are a few blurred images. It's like looking at mud under shattered glass. Where did I go for that violent duration? Where did I go?

We forget how delicate the phenomenon of consciousness can be, how we take it for granted. We sleep, we wake up. Through much of the night, however, while dead to the world, something else is going on—we are *dreaming*. All of us. Four or five times a night on average. Which means we are often talking, thinking, gesticulating, calculating, reacting, emoting, deciding, running, flying, fighting, witnessing, understanding. Yet so often we say with astonishing confidence, "I never dream." So, from one day to the next, nothing has changed, has it?

But sometimes while we sleep—this is the truth—amazing things happen. Maybe the roof is torn off our little dormitory, the floorboards are ripped up, and what we thought was solid planking beneath our feet, and a stable heaven over our heads, turns out to be more elusive than solid ground and clear sky. By turns chambered or tunneled, rocky or airy, burning or flooded, dream-space is inhabited space, even when it looks like "nothing" to us dreamers. *Nothing, after all, is also something.* French philosophers even have a name for the nothingness: They call it *le néant.* The void. And beyond the nothingness? *Au-delà du néant?*

What then? But let the French philosophers have their way with categories. For, whatever guise dream-space takes, be assured that if you penetrate it to sufficient depths, you will find that it is always active, always shaping, forming, crafting, anticipating . . .

Though stripped of memories like a vault ransacked by thieves, those devastating twelve-to-fourteen hours—for me—have never stopped surging and clanging, howling and ringing. I could not have known it then, but I would spend the rest of my life listening to the clamoring and whispering beneath the floorboards, and to the howling and whistling in the sky. I would be trying to discern what it was I lost, how the loss might also have been a gain, and what I would have to do and become as a result of that loss, and that gain.

THE NEXT TWENTY-FOUR HOURS I WAS NOT THE ONLY PATIENT in this hospital. There were patients in the three other beds, surrounded by family members talking quietly. Someone woke me and gently asked me if I could take a spoonful of broth in my mouth. I raised my head, which felt heavier than yesterday. Most of my head had been wrapped in gauze. I imagine a red stain seeping through the white wrappings, where my right eye had been, though I had no mirror, and no once was standing over my bed describing my appearance. My front tooth was broken, others chipped. The nose was also broken—for the second time—and further deformed by gauze packing. At least they saturated the gauze with Vaseline. I lowered my head and drifted away, sinking beneath pounding waves.

"Bob, wake up. Wake up!" It was Phil speaking. "What's your mother's phone number?" *Mother? Phone number?*

I struggled to comprehend what Phil was saying. Finally, I produced a series of numbers, and Phil left.

Sometime later, a nurse—*una enfermera*—spoke to me soothingly, offering me some cubes of red jello. I weakly chewed a cube or two, then slipped off again, into quieter depths. Phil returned sometime later. He said, "We ran into a cow. You hurt your eye, but they say it will be fine"—which was a lie, of course, though I didn't know it yet. It was only in retrospect that I realized they were lying to me, because the eye no longer existed except as a memory, or an impression in the gel of a black and white photo. At that point it was a gob of lacerated tissues, already infected, surrounded by broken bones, covered by gauze. The bandages helped staunch the bleeding, but that was about it.

Shortly after the collision during the night, as Phil drove us down the empty highway toward Caborca, he pulled over and stopped at a small building by the side of the road, honked the horn to rouse the occupants, got out and shouted for a doctor: *"¡Médico, médico!"* I remember hearing that, despite my delirium at the time. Apparently, I climbed out of the car and stumbled around before Phil put me back in. I don't remember that. I got the news later on, second-hand. The disturbed occupants of the shack, or whatever it was—had they been asleep?—pointed down the highway toward Caborca. Phil leaped into the VW and we took off. I passed out—or lapsed back into amnesia.

Outside of town we stopped at a cement factory or warehouse. Sodium vapor lamps in front of the building produced a dull yellow light, like an arsenic fog spreading heavily over the cratered parking lot. We rolled up to a loading dock and Phil shut off the engine. "Oh, God, my head hurts," I moaned. "Hang on, I've got to find help," said Phil. The sudden silence and stillness, under the buzzing sodium lamps, seemed as painful as the noise from the engine and bouncing of the car had been. My head throbbed violently. "Hurry up, Phil, hurry up!" I muttered to myself. I could hear the metallic ticking and tinging of the hot little engine as it cooled.

Phil returned, and we made our way in the battered bug to a small concrete building several blocks away. I later learned it had a large, square, red cross on the front—the *Cruz Roja de Caborca*. It was probably somewhere between 2:00 and 3:00 AM, but fortunately someone was on duty. Responding to Phil's pleas, the Red Cross attendant helped Phil load me into an ambulance, and soon they had deposited me at the small, four-bed Caborca hospital.

I say "hospital," but perhaps we need a different historical reference. This probably did not qualify as a hospital in the modern sense. In my imagination, reverie conjures up a dusty surgeon's tent during a Civil War battle, before the advent of modern anesthetics or antibiotics, where shot-up soldiers were brought in on stretchers and wagons. In those days, I imagine that the main tools in the doctor's medical kit were whiskey, tourniquets and bone saws. Maybe some laudanum, if the soldiers were lucky.

There was no whiskey tonight, however, and apparently no anesthetics. They could hardly apply a tourniquet to my neck to stop the facial bleeding, and enough sawing had already been done on my face anyway. The best they could do was to hold me down—Phil later told me it took four people in all, including Phil and the ambulance driver—and to pour some alcohol into the wound. Someone took a stab at sewing up the gashes with what was later described to me as "heavy black cord." I never saw it. They managed to pack the broken nose with gauze and to wrap the entire face and much of my head, but more than this was not possible. It was my good fortune that a bed was available. It was also my good fortune that Phil was not injured, since he was able to spend all of the next day *saving my life*.

The Mexican police impounded Phil's car for three days so they could conduct an investigation.

Thus, my brand-new, unseasoned guitar was locked in back of the black VW in the September Sonora sun for at least three days. Inevitably, the guitar swelled, shrank and warped, until some of the wood glue-joints had buckled and cracked open. Part of the lesson.

Given a choice between staying at the Red Cross or staying in the jail, Phil chose the Red Cross. In the meantime, he had to find a way to get me out of that hospital. So, mustering what Spanish he had, he began threading his way through the maze of Mexican legalities: filing a police report, securing a signature for a medical release, finding air transport—a Piper Cub crop duster—and a pilot named José. Phil phoned my mother in California, choreographed plans for her to hire a plane, fly to Tucson and taxi across the border to pick me up at the Mexican airport in Nogales.

Through all this frenzied activity Phil's body was also ravaged, though he was technically uninjured. But the lack of sleep, the drumming of caffeine through his veins, the craziness of trying to do everything in Spanish, the deadly pressure, must have torn him into virtual pieces, as if he was a human document run through a shredder, then glued back together with caffeine and adrenaline.

Meanwhile, I may as well have been rolling in a boat on the deep blue billows somewhere off Circe's Island. Late that afternoon, Phil woke me again. Two other men were with him. Phil told me to get out of bed and walk outside, where he told me I was going to be flown to Nogales. I could hardly complain, since I could hardly talk. They ushered me out of the hospital, into the full force of the Sonora sun. I don't know what the temperature was, but it felt like 110 degrees F. It wasn't exactly like breathing flames, but it was something along those lines. José the pilot would drive me in his open-cockpit, Model A Ford roadster to the Caborca air strip. From there he would fly me to Nogales, Sonora, on the Mexican side of the border.

Everything was happening too fast for me. My headache permitted little tolerance for anything but sleep. Once José and I were airborne, the heat, the noise and jostling of the small plane, the feeling of being endlessly suspended in mid-air. I didn't know if I could stand it, but what choice did I have?

Within fifteen minutes or so of my arrival at the airport in Nogales, my mother walked into the small waiting room, where I sat on a concrete bench in a dull stupor. She was accompanied by three men—the pilot from California, the taxi driver from Arizona and a friend who had agreed to accompany her on the flight.

After a few formalities, she paid José the fifty dollars he charged for the air transport, and we all said good- bye. I shook José's hand and thanked him. The solemn entourage then squeezed me into a yellow taxi, and we crept through stifling heat and heavy traffic, inching toward the border, to the airplane waiting twenty miles away, on the northern outskirts of Nogales, Arizona.

That night, on the return flight over Arizona to California, the small aircraft struggled across the entire desert, flying against powerful headwinds and thunderstorms still sweeping in from the Pacific. It felt like the plane was not really moving forward, just dangling in the wind, like a bucket on a chain over a furnace. But finally, we cleared the last of the mountains and touched down around midnight at the Fullerton airport in Orange County. I stepped out of the plane, climbed down a short ladder onto the tarmac and stood in the cool night air. I managed to keep my balance and stay on my feet. I still had the headache, but the cool air was a relief.

The next day was given over to doctors, antibiotics, surgery. For three days I lay in a drugged, tormented slumber, tossing and sweating. My only memories of that time would be of dreams, with images of slashing storms at night, dark clouds, wind and lightning.

I woke up early the third day. I was alone in the hospital room. My head was relatively clear. For some reason, I held up my hand and looked at it. It was flat. This was a hint that, from now on, things would be very different. Carefully putting my feet on the floor and finding I could stand and walk, I shuffled in paper hospital slippers to the bathroom. My nose was packed with fresh gauze, but the wrappings around my head had been reduced to a simple gauze patch over my eye, held in place with surgical tape. I stood in front of the bathroom mirror, took the tape between my fingers and gently pulled. The tape released its hold and the white patch fell away. For the first time since the accident, I was able to see what had happened to me, superficially at least. I looked at the face staring back at me from the mirror. Where my right eye had been, there was now a red concavity. Taut sutures tied in little knots ran here and there across the face, above and below the socket. My new task would be to learn how to see the world from the perspective of my left eye only. Not surprisingly, I had no clue what that might mean.

One day as I lay in the hospital bed, studying the patterns on the acoustical tile ceiling, Phil walked into the room. He had driven non-stop from Caborca to the hospital where I was being treated. And here he stood, my school-yard friend, yesterday a boy, today a man. How much did he age since the night of the accident? Years? However, you do the math, there was no doubt that the person who approached my bed was endowed with great courage.

Lying there in the hospital bed, I still knew very little about what had happened. Phil told me what he could about the accident, filling in some of the enormous blanks. A lot of it was a blur to him as well. Then he handed me a small black-and-white photograph showing all the Red Cross ambulance drivers of Caborca, in uniform. They had thoughtfully given it to him before his departure and had written an inscription on the back of the photograph: *"Para nuestro buen amigo Felipe White, un sincere recuerdo de los ambulantes de la Cruz Roja de Caborca."* For our good friend Philip White, a souvenir from the ambulance drivers of the Red Cross of Caborca. Then their signatures: Carlos Pino, Billy Ortega, Leonardo Elias Jaime, Luis Jaime, Juan Antonio Rivera, Miguel Angel Morales, Germán Contreras Pino, Jornulfo Gómez, Felipardo Martínez Callezda, Ricardo Partillo, and Paulino Sánchez.

So many names and faces, and I knew none of them. Yet someone from this list had risen up in the middle of the night to carry the wreckage of my body to the hospital, had stood fast amidst the blood and the screaming, had given Phil a bunk to sleep in, fed him, been kind to him, helped him make his way through the complexities of the situation, given him what succor he could. And for this he received no pay: the *ambulantes* were volunteers.

I stared at the photo, the khaki uniforms, the sunglasses, the white building, the red cross. There was no way I could know where the photo would one day take me. I only knew that I intended never to cross that border again.

Though decades have passed since that accident, it has never been far from my mind. I did not know it at the time, but Caborca marked me. I was like someone who had been branded, partly because of the livid scars, the alteration of my entire face. But also, because I had been somehow *singled out*. In one violent blow I had been torn out of my complacent identification with the mass of people and cast with no warning or preparation into the depths of my own isolated experience. I had become what Herman Melville called one of the "isolatoes."

Caborca, then, was my initiation into a mystery—or rather, the mysteries. But far from being just a starting point, Caborca also gradually came to symbolize an overarching pattern of meaning that followed me throughout many subsequent decades, as if there was some Active Intelligence, some transcendent agency, working both in me and in the world— now boxing me in or pulling me up short, now stretching me out and challenging me, now making demands.

It was as if a stake had been driven into the ground, and I was a bird tied to that stake. Whenever the bird tried to walk or fly, the limiting tether always pulled it back *toward the center*. Seen from above, all the tangential movements and exertions of the bird created, over time, a circular scrollwork rosette in the dirt, an accidental, improvised—yet mysteriously ordained—life-mandala. Every minute scratch revealed all the more forcefully the overwhelming presence of the *center*, and its patterning influence.

Caborca has had for me the quality of *fate*. It established certain defining limits of my life. At the same time, it also yielded a powerful sense of *destiny*, because it led me to a revelation of the goal implicit in those limits. Paradoxically, both the limits and the goal, the fate and the destiny, have opened up a widening range of inner potentials I might never have learned about had I not been brought so close to death and been awakened so violently.

The loss of my eye in Caborca, then, was the catalyst for an abrupt shift in my way of seeing, and not just physically. Overnight I was a different person, and I had much to learn about who that person was.

Suddenly, words like insight, outlook, perspective, vision, focus, point of view, depth perception, clarity, obscurity, shadow, illumination, liminal, sub-liminal and so on, took on a burning importance, as if from now on they would dominate my approach to the world.

I began this story with an account of the accident, but it is not my purpose to dwell on it. Nor do I wish to tell the story of "my life to date." Both the accident and my life simply provide an armature over

which to add some clay, in order to shape the more important story. For out of the aftermath of the accident, and the effect it had on my personality and life, there grew an unusual series of experiences and insights, and *it is to these latter that I must bear witness*.

In the final analysis, my life is a small thing, but this story is about something greater: the limiting, defining, centering force that, over and over, implicated me in its inscrutable designs. As I hinted in the Prologue at the outset, the whole process brought me close to the gates of heaven, and the gates of hell, at each of which I feel like I might have caught a few evanescent, flashing glimpses of something hinting at the divine.

C. G. Jung once wrote:

> If God wishes to be born as man and to unite mankind in the fellowship of the Holy Ghost, He suffers the terrible torment of having to bear the world in its reality. It is a crux; indeed, He Himself is His own cross. The whole world is God's suffering, and every individual human being who wishes even to approach his own wholeness knows very well that this means bearing his own cross. But the eternal promise for him who bears his own cross is the Paraclete.[2]

PART TWO
Lunar Vision

No one should deny the danger of the descent, but it
can be risked. No one need risk it, but it is certain
that someone will. And let those who go down the
sunset way do so with open eyes, for it is a sacrifice
which daunts even the gods. Yet every descent is
followed by an ascent; the vanishing shapes are
shaped anew, and a truth is valid in the end only if it
suffers change and bears new witness in new
images, in new tongues, like a new wine that is put
into new bottles.[3]

—C. G. Jung

IN THE TRADITION OF SYMBOLS, THE RIGHT EYE IS THE SUN-EYE, and the
left eye is the Moon-eye, another way of saying, "solar vision"
and "lunar vision." The right side is what our culture values,
the left side it generally mistrusts. The Latin word for right,
dexter, yields the English "dexterity," whereas the Latin word
for left, *sinistra,* yields the English "sinister."

In Norse mythology, when Odin, who was always seeking
wisdom, arrived at the Well of Urd, lodged among the roots of
the world-tree, *Yggdrasil*, it was guarded by *Mimir*, who was in
the habit of partaking of its magic waters. Odin told Mimir he
came for a drink of the sacred water. Mimir informed him
what it would cost: *the sacrifice of his right eye.* This was the
price he had to pay, the sacrifice he had to make, to attain

29

inner vision. And so he did, gouging out his right eye and dropping the sacrificed organ into the well. Whereupon Mimir dipped his horn into the waters and offered Odin the drink he'd earned. Thus, Odin attained wisdom—that is, *inner vision,* or the ability to see into the dark. By this sacrifice he gave up the conventional views valued by the many and adopted the more obscure perspectives of the interior way, valued by the few.

To me, the mythic pattern of "Odin at the Well" shows the possibility of personality transformation through the *conscious sacrifice of collective attitudes.* The accident in Caborca shows what can happen when the sacrifice is demanded of a *somnolent ego,* as mine was. If the individual is asleep to the greater forces that are calling to him or her from out of the darkness within, then when it comes time to transform, the sacrifice will take place *unconsciously,* and by often forcible means.

In pursuing the conventional path of my youth during the years "B.C." (before Caborca), I followed the "well-worn paths" of the herd, and I willingly, if unconsciously, conformed to the "solar" outlook of the age, tending to see mostly the external, superficial and rational aspects of things—their materiality, as it were. My dreamier side was present to me, I now realize, but in a state of relative neglect. It was for this state of affairs that the accident in Caborca served as a *corrective.*

In the years since Caborca, I have been forced to develop that dreamier, more lunar perspective, forced to abandon the straight line, the well-worn path of convention, and follow instead the crooked, unorthodox, serpentine path of individuation.

Of course, I didn't know any of this at the time. I just lost my eye and changed. I just felt different. I looked in the mirror and *didn't know who I was.* I found myself seeking solitude where before I had sought companionship; entertaining serious thoughts where before I had been all for joking; reflecting where before I had simply reacted. I essentially turned my gaze inward, and discovered there a world of feelings, emotions, images, ideas, intuitions, insights and longings I did not know I possessed, and that were scarcely recognized by the world around me. I had awakened. I had become a problem to myself.

Phantom Vision

AFTER I WAS RELEASED FROM THE HOSPITAL IN CALIFORNIA, but before returning to Stanford to begin my senior year, I spent a week at home. It was *an interim week, a fallow period* given over to recovery. The surgery and antibiotics were doing their jobs, and all that remained was to give the orbital tissues and bones a chance to heal, the swelling time to subside, attend a couple of follow-up medical appointments, and the like. Take it easy, think about my upcoming class schedule. And since I was only twenty years old, and in pretty good athletic shape, I assumed I was just banged up, like when my nose was first broken, playing soccer.

Or so I thought.

During that interim week I had a strange experience. I was looking in the hall closet for something and hadn't bothered to turn on the hall light. As I leaned into the total darkness of the closet, I felt an eerie sensation. I felt like I was seeing something in the dark . . . *with my right eye*! I quickly recognized the phenomenon of the "phantom limb," a ghostly experience common to anyone who has lost an arm, a leg, a hand, a foot, etc., to trauma. So, this was "phantom vision" I was experiencing!

I mention this event now because "phantom vision" serves as a *suitable metaphor* for the shift in perspective that was taking place within me back then. As a result of the accident, I was now to experience "binocular" vision—including something akin to depth perception—*only when I looked into the darkness*. In the fullness of daylight my vision would be literally halved. Seeing into the dark with only my left eye, activated *intuitive potentials* I didn't know I had. Intuition amounted to a *different, almost extra-sensory, supplemental kind of vision* that I had actually been capable of before Caborca—since childhood, I now realize. But I had to be dragged to the brink of death in order to wake up to the real potentials it offered—*to become conscious of them.*

Today, I regard intuition as one of the great, mysterious gifts of life, an innate potential ready to be developed, an enrichment, a skill from which anyone can benefit, and which could allow anyone to be of unusual service to the world—assuming they have not lost the innate impulse to serve and cooperate.

Obviously, intuition is not the only basis for humane service, by any means, but we are as much in desperate need of its rare gifts, as we are in need of rare metals. This general lack, ironically, might be most apparent to other intuitives, who feel its absence in the current ways of the world.

Intuitives who are alert to the gift it presents, may often experience a dilemma: *How can we possibly know something without also knowing where the knowledge came from, to trace its causal pathways, like normal people?* But that's how intuition is, an epistemological mystery. My experience suggests that intuitive knowing comes to us the way dreams come to us. But where do *they* come from? The gurgling tubes and wires of the brain-as-machine? Reductive materialists like to assume that something like thoughts and intuitions are a metabolic result of brain chemistry, a little chem-lab chuffing away inside our crania—*nothing but the random interactions of matter.* But if we are honest, we cannot really say with rock-solid certainty where dreams and intuitions come from.

I prefer more of a "cautious," depth-psychological formulation: Intuition comes to us from the depths of the "unconscious," wherever that is. I take it a step further: Intuitions can come to us from within or from without, as *fields of knowing,* very similar I imagine to the ancient experience of *gnosis* (Gr. for "knowing"), or *sophia* (Gr. for "wisdom"), but free from strict doctrines. And whether I am rationally justified in the following assumption or not, I even suspect that *intuition is part of our animal inheritance,* an aspect of instinct—as much as walking, running, dancing, singing, playing, fighting, eating, loving, nurturing, hunting, seeking the comfort of a warm nest, curiosity and its explorations, and so forth. Intuition is a basic, given propensity of our nature.

I cannot imagine life without intuition. And yet it seems that many or most of us disregard its whispered potentials as we yield to the whip of training. How often have we heard or read it confidently proclaimed: "We need more education in math and science!" I cannot remember the last time, if ever, I heard someone proclaim: "We need more intuition, more poetry and art!"

In case it's not obvious, I should mention that my comments about intuition naturally incline toward *the introverted side of intuition*. Yet, I recognize that entire fields of intuitive endeavors can be found in extraverted activities as well, where our intuitions alert us to outer potentials—*what lies over the next hill*, so to speak—of much use to real estate developers, inventors, fashion marketers, stock speculators, etc. And since we place so much emphasis on the various forms of extraversion, this type seems to be far more prevalent than introverted intuition—plus it usually pays a lot more.

Jung, who was also an introverted intuitive, but with a strong thinking-function, once made a revealing comment about *introverted intuition*:

> The perception of the images of the unconscious, produced in such inexhaustible abundance by the creative energy of life, is of course fruitless from the standpoint of immediate utility. But since these images represent possible views of the world which may give life a new potential, this function [introverted intuition], which to the outside world is the strangest of all, is as indispensable to the total psychic economy as is the corresponding human type to the psychic life of a people. *Had this type not existed there would have been no prophets in Israel.*[4] [Emphasis added.]

So, I espouse introverted intuition as it comes to me, intermixed with feeling-values: It is my ocean. I am a fish, breathing in its strange waters. I am only too aware that most of us are *trained to ignore it.* Yes, we are taught to *think, think, think,* but not generally taught to *intuit, intuit, intuit.* So, introverted intuition is one of the left-handed, "sinister" paths we regard with mistrust. Combine this suspicion with my disfigurement at Caborca and my subsequent psychological upheaval, and my well-developed feeling of being a *rara avis,* a rare bird, begins to make sense.

Here is another curiosity about intuition: Even though I just called it "part of our animal inheritance," I don't think it can be always and forever reduced to an *animal instinct* in the flesh and bone, sex and saliva sense, the strictly materialistic, only biological, "mechanistic" sense that has been so popular for so long. Intuition also, or maybe primarily, also has an immaterial, "volatile," spiritual aspect to it, which is probably why the alchemists so often used the image of the dragon, or winged serpent—in their manuscripts. It belongs both to the earth and the sky at once.

For all that I decry the reductive materialistic viewpoint, which I think still prevails, I also recognize—gratefully—that there is a current trend that is lightening up on the *absolutism of materiality.* In fact, in the early 20th-century, the eminent British mathematician and cosmologist Sir James Jeans made this intriguing statement:

> The stream of knowledge is heading towards a non-mechanical reality; the Universe begins to look more like a great thought than like a great machine. Mind no longer appears to be an accidental intruder into the realm of matter We ought rather hail it as the creator and governor of the realm of matter.[5]

For most creative artists and writers, it seems that intuition is desirable, perhaps even a virtual necessity. When I talk to my neighbor, a retired chemical engineer *who actually understands quantum physics*, and I ask him about the latest quantum theories, he talks, and I listen—but I listen with my intuition. My thinking function being quite inferior to my intuition, I follow him in much the way a faithful dog follows its master—with its nose. I follow the invisible "scent" of those abstruse quantum arguments, as the words burst into images in my mind as it tags along, tail wagging.

Things Will Be Different Now

> There is no coming to consciousness without pain.
>
> —C. G. Jung

ONE DAY DURING THE INTERIM WEEK, Phil unexpectedly pulled up in front of my house. The repairs had been carried out on his VW, thanks to the *noblesse oblige* of the Mexican magistrate, who gave him permission to drive to Nogales alone, on his own cognizance, with a verbal promise to return, while still under police jurisdiction in Caborca. Nogales had sufficient auto-body facilities to do the repairs he needed to be able to drive his car back to California. They did a reasonable job of piecing the car back together, under the conditions and time constraints. So, there we were, back in the semi-arid, mid-September, golden California sunshine, standing by his VW in front of my house. I'd been patched up and Phil's car had been patched up. Except for my one missing eye, everything had been restored to the *status quo ante*, right?

I don't recall any special purpose for the visit by Phil, except to re-connect with me one last time, after our hellish experience in Mexico, and before we returned to our respective colleges—he to UCLA, I to Stanford. We had only spent a half-hour or so together in the hospital, when he gave

35

me the ambulance-drivers' photograph. He hadn't even been to his own home yet. So, this visit would be our last chance for a *final handshake between friends after a shared hardship*.

But there was a degree of *tension* between Phil and me that had never existed before. Something was different. Stilted. Lots of nervous grinning, as I recall. Jokes that weren't funny. I now wonder if we were trying to regain what had come so easily to us in the past. I had no animosity at all towards Phil, nor he toward me, to my knowledge. I knew then, as I still know today, over half a century later, that in effect he saved my life. What else could I feel toward him but love and gratitude? And that was certainly true.

And yet, a *rupture* of some sort had taken place between us, and it was not just the bones in my face, or the glass in his windshield that had been fractured. But what was it? I didn't realize how painful it was.

There was neither time nor circumstance to find out. No ironing out of whatever wrinkles had developed between us— had we even known what they were. I think now that something *far greater* than the two of us had taken the reins and was now in control. For my part, it was as if a price were being demanded from the *undifferentiated unit* we had been before—two inseparable pals joking around as one, finishing one another's sentences, inventing silly, make-believe radio skits. A price was being extracted, then, a *value* removed from where it had previously been invested, psychic energy that needed to be *reinvested* elsewhere, like Jung's earlier metaphor of new wine in new bottles. Or think of the way a smooth eggshell has to crack and break, in order for whatever life is *growing and differentiating inside the egg*, to be released.

Looking back on that interim week, so hard on the heels of the actual accident, it later occurred to me that, without my knowing it, a revelation was already under way. I had undergone what must have been a personal *apocalypse,* in the original sense of the Greek verb, *apokaluptein,* "to reveal, to uncover." The cover had been ripped off my personality in Caborca, as if the sparkling veil of shallow cheerfulness that had previously lain so softly upon me had been rudely yanked aside, in order that something else could be revealed. But at the time I could not consciously register the fact that something earth-shaking had happened to me in Mexico.

Meanwhile, it was back to the university. When I arrived at the campus, I drove up behind the fraternity house where I had been living before Caborca. I'd been quite content as part of a group of intelligent people that I liked. I pulled into a parking space and got out of my car. Classes wouldn't begin for a few days yet, but students were beginning to drift onto the campus. One of my fraternity brothers came up to greet me as I got out of the car. I still had surgical tape on my face, and the whiskers were still growing through the mesh fabric of the tape. There was still a white gauze patch over my missing right eye.

This was the first fraternity "brother" I met face-to-face. I was surprised to find myself reacting to him with what felt like *embarrassment*. Apparently, I didn't know "how to act" after losing an eye, as I tried to resume my former place in this small, fraternal society. For his part, he looked at me with what struck me as a blank stare, a look of stupefaction. Maybe he too was embarrassed and didn't know what to say. Or maybe he just never said very much. I couldn't tell. In any event, neither of us said very much.

At the end of the previous spring term, I had felt comfortable here, a normal, two-eyed "brother." But now, returning in the fall with one eye and a scarred, lopsided face, I felt like an alien. Had I been more aware, more conscious, I would have realized that my discomfort at not knowing "how to act," was a clue that, before Caborca, I had been "acting." Besides, if I didn't know who I was *after* the accident, didn't that also mean that I didn't really know who I was *beforehand*? Maybe my previous sense of identity was just not deeply enough rooted, not authentic enough, to survive the severity of the collision.

It soon became clear that I could not abide living in my former social circumstances, so I moved out of the fraternity house and camped out in a small shack in back, sleeping on a couch. I also immediately quit the Stanford cheerleading squad, of which I was a member. In both cases, I was learning

37

that I could not tolerate belonging to groups, that I suddenly felt like an outsider. There was nothing wrong with the groups—they consisted of truly extraordinary people. Intelligent. Capable. Impressive. Talented in so many ways. I loved (most of) them as brothers. Maybe there was something "wrong" with me. In any event, I simply did not seem to *fit* any more. My "shape" had changed.

The university classes were also groups, but the impersonality of the classroom provided more *cover* for whatever it was I needed in my "banged up" state. What I needed, I now realize, was *solitude*. So, as I devoted more and more time to the solitude of "the shack," I prepared to plunge back into my studies as I had in previous years.

However, once I began attending classes, taking on the usual 15-unit class load of study-assignments, it quickly became apparent that the combination of chronic headaches, eye-strain in my remaining eye and a new, unfamiliar sensitivity to light ("photophobia"), did not leave me the strength to carry a full 15-unit class load. I was a lot more "banged up" than I realized.

I dropped two classes and spent most of my study-time reading about Latin American geography, French Culture and Modern Art. During Winter Term I took a reading class, plowing through the atmospheric novels of Thomas Mann. *The Magic Mountain* was fascinating—*Der Zauberberg!*—and suited the isolating mood of strangeness that was overcoming me. It was as if I was Thomas Mann's naïve protagonist, Hans Castorp, listening to the arguments between the intellectual giants—the humanist Ludovico Settembrini and the Marxist Professor Leo Naphta—as they argued away their days at the tuberculosis sanatorium in the Swiss Alps—at Davos, no less. While the two tubercular intellectuals reclined on their *chaises longues* in the cold, dry, alpine air, and Hans Castorp looked on like a spectator at a tennis match, for my part I lay on my couch in the "shack," reading Mann's majestic texts, listening to exotic flamenco records and somber classical and impressionist musical masterpieces, in between examining the works of the tumultuous array of modern artists for an art history class titled, "From Impressionism to Surrealism"—

Cézanne, Manet, Monet, Rouault, van Gogh, Sisley, Picasso, Seurat, Klee, Tchelichev and so forth.

And, as if to darken further the tincture that stained the days of that still-raw period of my smashed-up life, I also read through the mysterious works of Franz Kafka and Sigmund Freud—a far cry from my book-deprived, blue-collar, childhood background. My alienation was complete. I couldn't really communicate with my own family, or with my university second-family, or even the "family" of my larger American culture. It didn't help that the Vietnam War was ramping up. From a draft classification of 1-A, I was eventually re-classified 4-F—unacceptable for medical reasons—a blessing that spared me the horrors of that bloody war. My local draft board didn't want grunts with one eye. Caborca had marked me so deeply that I felt as if a large bull's-eye had been painted on my back. I very much doubt I would have survived Vietnam, had I been drafted.

Athletically speaking, I could still play soccer, which I enjoyed, and volleyball. Each of those balls was big enough that, even with one eye and diminished depth perception, I could see it coming my way and still react in time, compensating to a degree for the loss of depth perception with *parallax*.[6] But smaller objects coming my way were different. For example, I could not catch a baseball the way I could before. If someone threw me even a soft lob, I would hold out my hands and the ball would hit me in the chest. That was strange. Nor could I hit a tennis ball, zooming my way, with any assurance—more often than not it was a swing and a miss. I couldn't even catch a key-ring someone might toss to me. Without a second eye—necessary for triangulating the distance to objects, especially moving ones, and especially in gauging fine tolerances, like threading a needle—depth perception in the common sense would prove to be a permanent problem, still very much with me to this day.

I resumed the gymnastics classes I'd been taking before, but I discovered a new handicap. Whenever I tried to execute a front or back flip on the trampoline—so easy before—as soon as I was upside down in mid-air, in rotation, I completely lost my orientation and would end up flailing off the webbing

39

and crashing down onto the floor. Before Caborca, I had a cat-like sense of balance and agility, but that had been permanently compromised by the eye-loss. I continued gymnastics to the extent I could—even conducted gymnastics classes while teaching at a private school after graduate school—but I had to give up the trampoline. No great loss in itself, really, but a sign of still more changes to come.

Looking into the Mirror

I MENTIONED ABOVE THE STRANGENESS, AFTER THE ACCIDENT, that attended the everyday routine of *looking into a mirror.* The first time was three days after surgery, when I first saw the open wound. During the fallow week I did not tamper with the dressings, so the whiskers slowly pushed their inexorable way through the tape. But once I was back in school and back in classes, looking in the mirror was a normal part of anyone's morning ablutions. Thus, I discovered the problem of *mirroring* as a new challenge.

In a normal conversation, when you look someone in the eye you can often tell whether they are "seeing" you or not, assuming they're not closing their eyes, fluttering their eyelids or looking off past your shoulder and into the distance. Since Caborca, my experience of being "seen" or "mirrored" by others was subtly jarring to me, since I could often tell intuitively—as I looked out from "behind" what remained of my shattered "social mask" or persona—that I was not really being seen by them. True, I had begun living in my darker depths, whereas before I had been skating along on bright surfaces. Thus, it became habitual for me to experience not being seen clearly, let alone deeply. Much of this was simply because of the facial damage I had sustained, especially the replacement of my natural eye with a prosthetic eye.

Disturbances to the persona-aspects of our interpersonal relations can go in both directions. I can easily imagine, for example, that, despite my forced efforts at sociability, my patched-up countenance, darkened from within by a deeper sense of things, might have been faintly disturbing to others. Even if it was only intuitive, this heightened awareness of *fields of social discomfort* was one psychological burden of the accident.

And it was not just the physical scars surrounding my lost-eye that people might have found disturbing. The scars healed noticeably within the first two years and have almost disappeared today. Nor was it the horror-movie, spooky-doll near-immobility of the prosthetic eye I had commissioned in 1965, and that came to fill the void of my original eye-socket. The prosthesis is acrylic, hand-made in several stages by a skilled technician, with an "iris" that matches my remaining iris to near-perfection. It's so good a match that a past employer of mine, who worked with me closely for eight years, never realized that I only had one eye, until one day I happened to mention it. He was surprised. I was surprised that he hadn't noticed.

So, the effect of the prosthesis is visible, but so subtle as to be virtually *subliminal*. The pupil never changes size, no matter what the ambient light level might be. Bright or dark, the pupil stays the same. The blood vessels (drawn by the prosthetist on a molded, white-acrylic surface with a red pencil) are also always the same, so the prosthesis never becomes "bloodshot," no matter how fatigued, sun-struck or wind-blown, hence reddened, the living eye becomes.

The prosthesis does not track in parallel movements with the remaining eye, although it does move slightly, but not naturally, which is why I compare it to the spooky-doll effect of horror movies. Think of a ventriloquist's puppet like Charlie McCarthy, who, though obviously a fabricated "dummy," nevertheless has jaws that clack open and shut, and eyes that can move together, mechanically, back and forth. So much importance attaches to the eyes, the proverbial *windows to the soul*. Even in Hollywood, the *Mecca of Artifice,* much attention is given to the eyes, especially in those hokey horror films. My prosthesis results in a partial occlusion of the windows to my soul; but perhaps a sort of discomforting compensation takes place through deep emotions being closer to the surface. I think of them as mostly due to PTSD, but partly due to a tremendous and beneficial augmentation of my inner life. I move among images and emotions that most people suppress or repress. There is a passage from the Dylan Thomas poem, "Ballad of the Long-Legged Bait," that captures well this feeling of depth:

> She longs among horses and angels, The rainbow-fish bend in her joys, Floated the lost cathedral Chimes of the rocked buoys.

I learned there was a saving grace in having lost my eye. Something was taken away, yes, but as if to make room for something else to be given—if only I could find ways of responding to the new, while surviving the dislocations of the old. To many, this might sound like so much academic theorizing, mere whinging self-pity or plain malarkey, were it not for the fact that it had all been powerfully *experienced*.

Which is why, for decades, I have known and confessed that, "losing my eye was unfortunate; but I have also learned that it was a great gift."

Flamenco: A Hidden Treasure

FORTUNATELY, AS IF IN ANOTHER COMPENSATION for these irksome physical limitations, within a year after Caborca I had taken up a study of the *flamenco guitar*. As I learned more about the intricacies and subtleties of flamenco music, I found the depth of my emotional capacity for creative expression increasing considerably. Since I had spontaneously begun learning to play the guitar the year before—chord progressions, basic strumming and plucking techniques, scales, etc.—which is why I eagerly bought the ill- fated instrument in Mazatlán, I knew a few techniques and had developed a passion for learning more. So, once I discovered the esoteric art of flamenco, while living alone in the shack, I succeeded in finding two different flamenco guitar teachers, and hit the ground running.

Flamenco turned out to be a great boon for me, since the somber, exotic scales and tones of the gypsy flamenco, sometimes known historically in Spain as the "music of the outcast," suited my deepening emotional mood perfectly, the mood of one who had been singled out by fate through the loss of an eye in a broken face. And since I was majoring in Spanish (and French), I loved everything Spanish about flamenco, especially the melodies and modal (Phrygian) scales of voice and guitar; the complex rhythms and counter-rhythms executed by singers, dancers and guitarists alike; the *palmas* or rhythmic hand-clapping of the onlookers—*los testigos,* or witnesses; the extended, improvisational *melismas* of the singers, perfect for expressing intense emotions; and the beautiful *poetry* of the sung verses, or *"letras."*[7] Flamenco poetry was my first experience of a still-living oral tradition of amazing depth and beauty. It offered an artistic cultural form that grew out of the same kinds of emotions I was going through, turning pain and isolation into heartbreaking beauty.

One of my teachers was a professional flamenco guitarist from San Francisco, whose stage name was *Niño Bernardo.* He was an excellent teacher, and he helped me a lot. Meanwhile, I assiduously combed through every record shop I could find, looking for records—vinyl LPs in those pre-Internet days, and occasional archival 45s, most of them recorded by the old, traditional singers. Since there was no Internet, no YouTube, nor even cassette tapes in those early days, finding flamenco music really was a quest. But within a year I had acquired the nucleus of a respectable collection of flamenco records, which grew throughout the decades, and I gradually made contact with other flamenco dancers, guitarists and singers.

During my Master's Degree year at Stanford, I met a different flamenco guitarist—a physicist who was attending a summer-long, high-energy particle-physics conference at the

Stanford Linear Accelerator, and who had just returned from a year in Spain, where he had studied flamenco guitar in Madrid with *Eugenio González,* a respected teacher of flamenco.

One day I ran into this physicist/guitarist on the athletic field, in the middle of his karate workout. He had originally been somewhat secretive about the music he had learned, but this one afternoon, quite to my surprise, he let me borrow his music books, to Xerox that whole years' worth of guitar lessons, which laid out the basic components of the various flamenco forms or *"palos,"* (*palo* means trunk or branch, like the trunks and branches of a genealogical "tree"). In those music notebooks, all of the most common flamenco *palos* (around thirty or so) were laid out in *tablature form,* known in Spanish as *cifra* for "number" or "cypher."

Cifra is an old form of musical transcription dating back to the 1400s, originally used for organ and lute music. It uses numbers instead of notes, to represent frets and therefore pitch; and in guitar music, it uses six lines to represent strings on the guitar rather than a *musical staff of five main lines with abstract notation.* With *cifra,* fingering on the guitar or lute can be quite graphically accurate. And since most flamenco guitar music is *not written down at all,* tablature offers a flexible, graphic system suitable for learning the highly improvisational musical styles of flamenco without an expert teacher present. This was especially helpful to me since I did not read music, never had the opportunity to live or study in Spain, where guitar teaching is traditionally carried out through mimicry—the master demonstrates a passage or technique, and the pupil tries to imitate it.

For many years after Stanford I was living in areas where there were few or no other flamenco artists.

Thus, with that pile of Xeroxed music in hand—an entire year's worth of guitar lessons with Eugenio González— everything was written down in his slightly eccentric tablature style, which did not indicate the timing or rhythm clearly (crucial in flamenco), but I managed to decipher it, like a Rosetta Stone. It was a godsend for me—a *gold mine.* Once I finally figured out the cryptic system, I could compare his lessons with the musical archive of all the different flamenco *palos* as revealed on the flamenco records and anthologies I had collected. Soon enough I arrived at a creditable, elementary understanding of this amazing art form. For years, I spent countless hours with my head buried in the speakers of my stereo, listening as acutely as I could to the archaic sounds of the singers, young and old, and to the many guitarists, the subtleties of their improvised accompaniments and the beauty of their *falsetas*, or melodic variations, on the guitar.

Over time, then, my knowledge of the music deepened, and through studying and teaching, I learned to write tablature as fast as I could write cursive English. The tablature helped me not only to teach flamenco guitar, using *cifra* as I had been taught, but also to deepen my grasp of the guitar itself—a fairly complex instrument. I was able to compose my own *falsetas* and solos, and to transcribe entire flamenco solo pieces, note for note, composed and recorded by legendary Spanish guitarists, many of them virtuosos. This immersion in the exquisite music of genuine masters gave me a profound appreciation for the artistic musical treasures of folkloric Spain. Today, of course, with computers, digital recordings, videos and so forth, flamenco has burst forth in a somewhat profaned, popularized, world-wide form. One of the secrets of "real flamenco," is that it is in fact a kind of *sacred music of the Spanish soul.* And in its best enactments, often conducted in private, it has all the qualities of an ancient, tribal ritual.

In Spain, flamenco families—and entire villages—still take great pride in the creativity and virtuosity of their most accomplished artists. But the pride really begins in the womb and the cradle, in the blood, in the encyclopedic depth of knowledge of simple workers, of aunts and uncles, grandparents and cousins, the *abuelos y abuelas, primos y primas*—singing, playing the guitar, dancing or accompanying with *palmas* and shouting encouragement—called *jaleo,* meaning roughly, "hell-raising." They all know the complex rhythms, the sophisticated, syncopated handclapping, or *palmas* (from, *palmadas*—in Andalucian Spanish the final "d" is not pronounced), and they all know the different *palos.* Generally, they not only recognize, but also insist, that anyone who sings, or dances, or plays the guitar, *do their very best, always,* even and especially, their own children. There is a simple Spanish proverb that expresses this communal-yet-individual pride in artistry:

En el campo,	In the fields,
Cantar bien, o cantar mal.	Sing well, or sing poorly.
Pero donde hay gente,	But where there are
people, *Cantar bien, o no cantar.*	Sing well, or don't sing.

Over the decades that followed, the artistic sub-culture of flamenco provided a different kind of society and culture in which I didn't feel like such an outcast. Or rather, it was *as* an outcast that I found a place, and my unusual passion for the Spanish language found yet another, deeper kind of home in the exotic, emotional beauty of *cante flamenco y cante jondo*—the "deep song" of the Spanish soul.[8]

One notable result of my flamenco life took place, again by accident, in 1968, during a small private flamenco party, or *juerga,* with some friends: an American flamenco guitarist, who also knew how to sing flamenco—a rarity—and his wife, who knew how to dance flamenco and do the intricate, rhythmic accompaniment of the *palmas*. They too had spent a year in Spain studying flamenco. We were having fun, and I jokingly said, in Spanish, "If I had been born in Spain, I would have wanted to be named *Paco*." In the festive spirit of the party they obliged by calling me *Paco* for the rest of the evening. Within two days, everyone I ran into was calling me "Paco." Something had jelled, the name had "stuck," and ever since then—more than fifty years—I've been known as "Paco Mitchell." Many years later a Spanish gypsy flamenco singer, Jesus Montoya, added to the nomenclature by dubbing me, *"El Gitano Rubio"*—the Blond Gypsy.

First Mentor

THE FOLLOWING YEAR AFTER MY RETURN TO STANFORD FROM CABORCA, I entered a Master's Degree program. That's when I connected with my first real mentor, apart from my high school Spanish and French teacher, who was a great teacher, but not a mentor *per se*. Or perhaps he was my proto-mentor and I just didn't know it. He may have been more *aware* than I realize. Ironically, once I graduated from high school, he quit classroom teaching to become a school counselor.

But my first real mentor was a woman who, simply because of who she was, with her elevated level of intelligence, experience and awareness, came to serve that mentoring function for me. Her name was Marlea, which, as I recall, she told me meant "Desert Rose" in the Apache language. Very exotic, I thought. She was a talented and cultured woman who moved among higher circles of the Stanford intellectual community, and yet she taught Special Education classes in the high school where I served my internship teaching Spanish. She told me that, in order to teach Special Ed., you had to want "to heal broken wings." In my many conversations with Marlea, she set my mind on fire. Through her inspiration I began to educate myself outside of the Stanford curriculum— once again, *extra ecclesiam*. During my master's degree year, I estimate that I read between 100 and 150 books on my own, apart from all curricula.

Another result of the "branded" separateness that Caborca had forced upon me, then, was that I found myself becoming a confirmed *autodidact*—which I am to this day. I thank Marlea for initiating that shift.

Also, it was Marlea Jacobs who wrote a letter of introduction on my behalf to the renowned scientist Gregory Bateson, with whom I was privileged to spend long hours deep in conversation when I lived in Hawaii, where I was teaching languages at a private school after Stanford. It was Bateson who, in 1967, first introduced me, in the most patient way, to the basics of cybernetic theory, of which he was an expert and a pioneer. On that foundation he introduced me to the phenomenon of "runaway feedback loops in nature."

This exposure would eventually have far-reaching consequences, adding a new layer of responsibility that continues today. Its effect was almost dreamlike, as if I'd been given another "key" to understanding that I would have to figure out how to operate.

In essence, for the first *ten years* after Caborca, even as I was grasping at tantalizing hints and chasing sparks, reaching for new ways of knowing and expressing myself—the old life, the old personality, the "actor," was collapsing around me. But "phantom vision" was indeed a valid metaphor, pre-figuring new abilities that were growing out of my loss and disfigurement.

At the same time, my difficulty with the trampoline was also a metaphor, as I said. It foreshadowed a different type of tumbling, flailing and falling—i.e., the collapse that I suspect was well underway even as I still lay unconscious in the tiny Caborca hospital. Altogether, the mounting sum of "wreckage" was confusing and painful, to me and to others close to me, difficult but necessary or, as Jung might put it, *ineluctable*—not to be avoided. In many ways my life had been reduced to rubble, like a demolished building whose wrecked materials are used to build the foundation for some new, as-yet-unrevealed structure to come—which is precisely an image that came to me in a portentous dream years later. All efforts to continue my former life of conformity or normality were understandable, but for the most part they all failed. In a sense, we could say I was undergoing a personal collapse which, in its greater, impersonal form, amounted to an *enantiodromia*—a Greek term for reversal, "a running to the opposite." The psychological process of *enantiodromia*, which can feel like one is being turned upside down, reminds me of the biblical saying:

> So the last shall be first, and the
> first last: for many be called, but
> few chosen.[9]

In terms of Jung's typology,[10] I had been trying to force my "dominant function" to fit the collective mold, which, for most American men, probably tends toward *extraverted thinking* and *sensation*. In retrospect, post-Caborca, I now see that was a huge mistake on my part. I only realized over a period of years that my natural typology was not extraverted thinking and sensation at all, but rather *introverted intuition and introverted feeling,* with a heavy emphasis on art and creativity in general. Basically, I had been trying to adapt to the world through my weakest functions. One of the "purposes" of the accident in Caborca, then, was to turn me *upside down*, typologically speaking, and force me to rely on my most natural, most authentic functions of introverted intuition and feeling, which reportedly comprise about *2% of the American population!* No wonder I felt like such an "outcast." The further away I got from the assumptions and attitudes of my fellows, the closer I felt to myself. I was being dragged downward, reduced by that unknown but *ineluctable force* that was far broader, deeper and more powerful than my ego-personality.

But I am writing this with the benefit of many years of hindsight. At the time, all the changes happening to me were beyond my understanding. I had to lose virtually everything that had previously been dear to me, before I could begin to fit some of the puzzle-pieces together. Thus, *it wasn't until I found myself divorced, bereft and living alone in a different state—in a town where I did not know a soul*—that things really began to move.

Despite my deep chagrin, I welcomed the opportunity to start my life over on a different basis. But what basis was that? I later learned that the very question bespeaks an *epistemological crisis* in itself—the crisis of not knowing what your life is based on, of not knowing how you come to know whatever it is you think you know. Insofar as you *only* rely on the common knowledge of conformist society—those *groups* I found myself forced to avoid—you will probably learn very little about your actual, unique individuality—in a word, your *soul*. You can learn all about collective paths, assumptions, prejudices, knowledge, frameworks and molds. You can garner all the awards, degrees, credentials and honored positions, to be sure—what the crowd applauds—and even be *handsomely rewarded* for all those things. But to garner those treasures requires *conformity to and identification with the collective,* in one form or another, to one degree or another.

Jung had a trenchant observation to make about this aspect of society and its collective validations:

> There is a great temptation to be what we appear to be, rather than what we actually are, because the persona is usually rewarded in cash.

To explore the complex mystery of what I am calling "one's unique individuality," other means, methods and paths are required. That's what Jung was talking about—to become what we actually are—and it was what I needed to find. Thankfully, I was hell-bent on finding whatever "it" was. A lukewarm approach would not do.

It had to be something *creative*, and it had to involve my *hands*, but also using my *mind* and my *imagination*. There had to be *music-making, shaping things, imagining things*, and so forth. I resolved to go as deeply into my inward self as I could go, to get to the "bottom," if that were even possible, to find out *whatever* or *whoever* I was, in the deepest sense.

A specific phrase came to mind in describing this need or desire I had—this quest for the unknown. I needed to find my *"irreducible necessities."* I wanted no more universities, no more curricula, no more professors, no more textbooks, no more "paths" laid out by others, nothing that was not generated out of my own being, my own inner necessity. I was on a quest, and *dreams proved to be the primary means.*

Into this personal learning laboratory I brought with me (1) a well-developed love of the flamenco guitar and its music; (2) an interest in photography and the darkroom, where images appeared "alchemically" from out of the darkness in their chemical trays; (3) a recent but keenly developed interest in ceramics and kilns, fire and clay, the shaping of things; (4) and a habitual reliance on my daily journal, in which I drew and wrote.

To these new interests that were growing out of my "collapse," like flowers out of rubble, a few more were added. Five additional pursuits were crucial to my quest. They came

50

tumbling into my life almost simultaneously, but since I can't describe them simultaneously, I'll put them into the order that occurs to me.

The first pursuit was a spontaneous decision to start recording my dreams. No one was modeling this for me. I knew no one who practiced this discipline. I had never read any books about "dreamwork"—so common today.[11] However, I had read a small, old book a year or two earlier, which probably planted a seed. I still recall the title: *The Psychoanalyst and the Artist,* by Daniel E. Schneider (1950). I only remember a brief passage in the book that mentioned a breakthrough that had come to the protagonist by way of a *dream*, which opened up for him a flow of blocked creative "libido." I suspect it was that image or scene–of the dream and its release of creative energy–that served me as a seed, prompting my eventual decision "out of the blue," to investigate my own dreams.

At any rate, every morning I would wake up with dream-notes I had scribbled during the night on an expendable spiral notebook by my bedside. Then, over coffee, I would transcribe the dreams into a series of hardbound, permanent notebooks, in which I fleshed out the details. Sometimes I drew diagrams or sketches to depict the dream configurations, or whatever else they prompted in my imagination.

I hadn't gotten very far into recording my dreams before I recalled a *chronic dream* from childhood that had haunted me for years, but that I had forgotten about:

> *I am exploring a network of underground caverns where a large gorilla lives. Inevitably the gorilla "finds" me and comes "after" me, that is, toward me, and just as inevitably I run terrified from the gorilla, at which point I wake up.* [End of dream.]

That dream recurred for six, maybe seven, years. My parents would not have been able to help me understand what was going on, even if I had told them the dream. It got to the point where I would wake up groaning, "Oh no, not the gorilla dream again!"

But now I see that my child's dream-descent into the tunnels where the gorilla lived, was probably a hint that I was *destined* to learn how to find my way into and around those tunnels as an adult.[12] Furthermore, I realized that, if only I could find and reconnect with the gorilla, *make friends with it,* so to speak, it or he or she might provide me with a kind of *guidance,* since the gorilla *lived* down there and *knew its way around*. This realization confirmed the intuition that my spontaneous decision to record my dreams was the right thing to be doing. Today I think of the dream-gorilla as my childhood introduction to the *Spirit of the Depths*, one of many such spirits, no doubt, mainly visible in dreams.

Since I had moved to a small, picturesque waterfront town on Puget Sound, I soon developed a morning ritual—recording my dreams while watching the sunrise over the water, along with the antics of the various water-birds, bobbing and diving, taking off and landing. As I sipped coffee and puzzled over the mysterious dream texts that were accumulating in my notebooks, I watched powerful tugboats pulling immense log-booms down from Canada to the mills in Puget Sound; container ships and tankers from across the oceans making their way to the shipyards and refineries in Seattle and Tacoma; battleships, destroyers and submarines headed for Bremerton; a local ferryboat shuttling back and forth across the Sound.

In summertime, if there was fog over the water, the unseen presence of large ships and small boats was signaled by their moving foghorns, vooming and tooting, while a nearby, red-painted nun-buoy clanged erratically over a shallow sand-spit. Sailboats came and went from the local marinas; and three stationary foghorns, maintained by the Coast Guard and strategically placed on separate promontories, sounded out their life-saving codes across the water—different pitches, numbers, and durations of notes—allowing the accompanying musical-ships and-boats to navigate safely through the mist.

It was a glorious location, with panoramic views of beaches, islands and the snowcapped, saw-toothed Cascade Mountain range in the distance—and it all provided many occasions for the deep healing I dearly needed. Also belonging to this regimen, *day or night,* was my habit of walking on the beach.

Into the Darkness Again

THE ADVENT OF THE *SECOND CRUCIAL PURSUIT* OCCURRED one evening, when I decided on impulse to drive down to a local park just after sunset, to walk in the dark from there down to the beach. On reaching the sand, I looked out toward the Sound. I could tell by the gentle lapping sound of the water that the tide was out. The sun had gone down in the west, the sunset hidden by tall bluffs of glacial debris, which, ten thousand years earlier, had been covered by a great sheet of ice a mile thick. The sky to the north still shone with fading pastel watercolors of gold, pink, aquamarine, purple—all fading and blending in the clear, darkening sky. The moon had either gone down as well or had not risen yet. Darkness was taking command.

Slowly, I walked away from the town. The farther down the beach I got, the darker became the scene before me. Soon the colors had disappeared, and the sky was virtually black. I knew from previous ventures that there were great driftwood logs on this beach, cast adrift from log-booms of long ago. The logs migrated like husky vagabonds from beach to beach with the storms and tides, and rested against the sandy bluffs.

Between the driftwood and the water, tangled strands of kelp and scattered clamshells, crab-shells and other debris, lay upon the sand, washed up on the beach. As I kept walking— slowly, because I couldn't see what was in front of me—I "saw" something nevertheless, in the darkness. It reminded me of my experience of "phantom vision" in the closet during the fallow week after Caborca, after the surgery.

I couldn't be sure what I was seeing, of course, or if it even *was* anything. A few faint lights sparkled far across the Sound, but they were too faint and far away to give me any hint of what was in front of me. I had seen black on black, and that was it. But just like the hall closet, it felt like I was *seeing something* in the darkness within the darkness.

Then the hair stood up on the back of my neck, and I stopped walking.

The blackness had shifted. Whatever this "something" was, it had moved. Blackness now *moving* upon blackness—an eerie experience. It was definitely alive.

I opened my "good" eye as wide as possible. Then the darkness moved again.

This time I *really* got a case of goosebumps (Spanish = *escalofrío*). I discerned that the moving blackness stood or hovered on top of something also black, that seemed to project out of the water. The lower shape was a black rock, I surmised, in the approximate form of a pyramid, though I couldn't be positive.

At first, I thought the uppermost shape might be a sea-otter, standing on a rock at low tide.

I took a few more slow steps. Then I raised my arms in a spontaneous gesture of gratitude and—I might as well say it— praise. For, whatever this living creature might be, I had nothing but gratitude, praise and admiration for it. And goosebumps.

I could discern the rock thanks to the dim twinkle of lights from across the Sound, reflecting on the water's surface. But the dark mass was too high above the rock to be an otter, which has short hind legs. Maybe it was an *eagle on the rock*. It was big enough. But to my knowledge eagles preferred to strike from the air in daylight. Besides, this creature was also too high above the rock to be an eagle, like the otter. It was *something else.* By now I could feel, in all its ambiguity, the presence of something powerful and important. What was it even *doing here* at this hour, besides standing on a rock at low tide?

Then suddenly a huge pair of dark wings flared out into the night and the creature, a very large bird, flew in a semi-circle to another rock farther back, another pyramid shape, still in the shallow waters but farther down the beach.

I kept walking, one very slow step at a time, arms still raised, murmuring what would have been a prayer had I belonged to a church. The great wings flared, and the enormous bird circled once again to another rock still farther back.

The bird and I repeated this formula a third time.

Again I approached, slower than ever, barely advancing, and again the bird's wings flared, but this *fourth* time it flew in the opposite direction, parallel to the beach, the way I had come. As it flew past me, there was just enough light from miles away across the Sound, to enable me to distinguish its dark profile. I saw the great wings beating slowly, I caught a faint glimpse of long legs trailing behind the body, and I saw what had to be a neck, head and beak coiled up at the front.

Then I heard a guttural squawk, and it was gone.

The next day I told a friend what I had seen. She said, "That was probably a Great Blue Heron," and the following day she loaned me a red-covered copy of *Birds of North America.* There it was. *Ardea Herodias.* The Great Blue Heron.

From the moment I first saw it in the dark, I was seized by what I later learned was one of the "power animals" in ancient cultures, a mythological creature, in essence, often regarded as a manifestation of divinity. It would take quite a while, however—years, in fact—for these kinds of realizations to coalesce in my awareness, and for the herons—I want to say— *to incarnate as presences* in my dreaming and waking life. I know that probably sounds inflated and grandiose, but I don't know how else I can say it, and still do justice to the experiences.

In the meantime, and from the outset, all I knew was that, from out of the darkness on the beach, something mysterious had laid its claim on me—similar to what had happened in Caborca.

Gradually I would fill in some of the gaps in my knowledge of this great creature, its intimate relationship to me, as well as its crucial role in deepening my sense of the meaningful purpose implicit in Caborca.

Sometimes, when I think back on that first ten-year, post-Caborca period of my life, I could say it was a slow-rolling cascade of disintegrations, out of which came a series of multi-leveled integrations. I say "slow-rolling" because, just as one sunrise follows another, we are all caught up in whatever our "daily grind" might be, as if we were millers patiently grinding the grist of our lives. More often than not, and if lacking a higher perspective, we don't see the pace or the trajectory we are on. Nose to the grindstone, vision blurred, we take it one step at a time. Rocks in a stream, like geology.

But also, like geology, there is that unpredictable phenomenon known as "catastrophism," wherein the trickling pace of pebbles in streams is upset by sudden floods, volcanic releases and such. Gentle polishing leads to crashing fractures, as the mountain gravitates toward sand—and the polishing begins all over again.

One of the things I find difficult to convey about this story was, after so many years of confusion, unraveling and collapse, how *fast* things really began to come together, when they did.

I've already mentioned the onset of my *attending to dreams*. That was sudden. One day I had never recorded my dreams. The next day, I was recording every single one I could recall, every day. And then there was my attention to the herons. One day, no herons. The next day, herons galore.

The Depth Psychology of C. G. Jung

THE THIRD CRUCIAL PURSUIT OCCURRED VIRTUALLY simultaneously with the advent of these first two passionate interests of dreams and herons: that is, *the depth psychology of C. G. Jung.*

The same friend who identified the heron for me and loaned me her "bird book," also loaned me her copy of Jung's autobiographical work, *Memories, Dreams, Reflections.* She put this book in my hand after I had told her about beginning to record my dreams, and also that I had come across a stunning quotation from Jung, whom I had never read before.

The book was electrifying. I had received a second Master's Degree, in Counseling Psychology, before moving to Puget Sound. However, I found the counseling courses to be dull and uninteresting. But reading that first Jung quote, which I had found while thumbing through the *Whole Earth Catalog,* set me on fire again (another fire experience, like the mentorship with Marlea, flamenco, the heron and the dreams).

The quotation spoke directly to the point in life I had reached, and said what I needed to hear, after all my thrashing around post-Caborca. Here is the initial quote from Jung:

> Anyone who wants to know the human psyche will learn next to nothing from experimental psychology. He would be better advised to abandon exact science, put away his scholar's gown, bid farewell to his study, and wander with human heart through the world. There, in the horrors of prisons, lunatic asylums and hospitals, in drab suburban pubs, in brothels and gambling-hells, in the salons of the elegant, the Stock Exchanges, socialist meetings, churches, revivalist gatherings and ecstatic sects, through love and hate, through the experience of passion in every form in his own body, he would reap richer stores of knowledge than text-books a foot thick could give him, and he will know how to doctor the sick with a real knowledge of the human soul.[13]

This passage led me straight to *Memories,* the autobiographical book my friend had loaned me, and constituted my introduction to Jung, who soon proved to be an unparalleled guide to dreams, to the world and history of symbols, and to the basic structure and dynamics of the psyche, at both conscious and, most importantly, at unconscious levels. I devoured *Memories, Dreams, Reflections,* and began reading as much of Jung's work as I could get my hands on.

As for my dreams, I noticed that, as I became more interested in, respectful of, and knowledgeable about them—thanks to Jung's guidance—*the dreams changed.* I recognized in this change a form of "responsiveness," a sense that the dreams were becoming *more purposeful and directed, less nonsensical and fragmentary.* I am even tempted to say that they began to exhibit a kind of *sentience* in themselves, as if the dreams were manifestations of something like a dynamic awareness, an *Active Intelligence,* coming to me while I slept, from whatever mysterious "place" dreams come from.

But the intelligence I saw in dreams was anything but static. Rather, it was a supremely dynamic, spontaneous intelligence that seemed to *know more about me than I knew about myself.* Dream intelligence was capable of weaving together the most stunning combinations of images in the most creative ways.

Weaving tapestries. Telling stories. Composing poetic images that seemed to embody potentials for my own awareness, and that extended far beyond my meager accomplishments.

To someone who has not experienced something similar, never bothered to investigate hundreds of their own dreams, I know that my reference to the "awareness" that resides in and among dreams may sound bizarre, but it's true: The more attention and respect I gave them, the more purposeful they became—*as if in response.* And I've seen it happen with other people as well. What begins as fragmentary, disconnected images, wacky and nonsensical, begins to reveal underlying motifs, interrelated over many dreams, like multi-colored glass beads on a string, or like a unique tapestry woven by a master-weaver.

Eventually, *herons* began appearing in my dreams. Taken together, as you might imagine, the heron dreams *formed their own series* over the years, a discernible leitmotif which, though taking its leisurely time, the way herons do, was nevertheless *going somewhere,* leading me further into the realm of the strange and mysterious.

However, what was so distinct about *every* heron dream was not the *number* of them, for they were few, perhaps fewer than a dozen. What impressed me then and impresses me still was their sheer, overwhelming, unforgettable *power and magnitude.* In some uncanny way, I would even say that the heron dreams were *majestic.* I have had many powerful, unforgettable dreams over the decades. But every time a heron presented itself in a dream of mine, as I considered the dream closely and carefully, each time I ended by regarding it as a "big dream." I never had a "small" heron dream. The herons, and the dreams that brought them, had *all* clearly come from the deeper reaches of the psyche—what Jung called the *collective unconscious* or the *objective psyche*—rather than from the more superficial layers, which he designated the *personal unconscious*. I had learned enough from reading Jung, and from recording and studying dreams, to be able to differentiate between those two types of dreams—personal and archetypal—as I followed the "back, down and in" trajectory of attending to dreams. Why did the herons enter my dreams from such inner depths, as if reaching up and out toward my consciousness? Why did they come to me at all? Was my first encounter with the heron on the beach that night *nothing but a chance, meaningless event and nothing more,* the way most of us were taught to think? Or did it prefigure something?

Incidentally, I never regarded the herons that appeared in my dreams as residual expressions of my daily experiences or personal quirks—i.e., I did not regard the heron dreams from a Freudian perspective—the "dust-bin" theory of dreams, where dreams are seen as *nothing but "day-residues."* Nor were they Freudian "wish fulfillments," or symptoms of "infantile sexuality" or the "Oedipal complex." On the contrary, the herons appeared in my dreams as great, archetypal presences, emissaries or ambassadors, sent from afar, from that ever-mysterious "somewhere else" of the objective psyche, but always bearing messages of import that bore directly on my character, my personality, my destiny and my fate. Furthermore, not only were they implicated in my life, but also—I am now beginning to imagine—they may also lead me to, or bestow a meaning upon, my death.

This may seem like a tall order for the reader to consider—that "mere dreams" might pertain to such an array of large, more-than-personal contexts. But I swear, there is no frivolous intent in what I'm saying. It is the result of serious application over decades. I don't pretend to lay claim to absolute truth, but I do know that my life has taken on more substantial depth of meaning, more inner dignity, through what I have suffered and learned, through the mistakes I have made, than I would have gained only through success on the world's terms. Sometimes secret knowledge, when it connects us with something greater than we are, is worth more than wealth.

When big dreams appear, they remind me of the way lava emerges on the surface of the earth, when the crust ruptures and molten magma surges upward, under pressure, through whatever fissures are within its reach. Who knows how many such potential psychic fissures exist in the world of humans in our billions?

Far more than we think, I'd wager. How different our world would be if there were more dream-seekers afoot! Why do we resist our dreams so? Are we so psychically benumbed that we really believe our dreams are worthless?

I have no doubt that the figure of the Great Blue Heron, as it appeared in my dreams, which eventually became interwoven with synchronistic events in my waking life,[14] was a manifestation of the objective psyche, an archetypal figure from the *mythopoeic* layers of the unconscious. To put it another way: Because of how the heron presented itself to me in those sleeping dreams and waking synchronicities, I eventually recognized the meaningful pattern of what the ancients called a *daimon*.

Heron As Daimon

DAIMON IS A GREEK WORD DERIVED FROM DAIESTHAI, "to divide" or "to distribute." It refers to a guiding, tutelary spirit or deity, a numinous presence, an angel. In pre-Christian understanding, the *daimon* was ambivalent, in that it could both harm and heal—cf. the six-foot-tall heron-man striking at my Caborca eye. Was that an invitation or a threat? The term *daimon* later became assimilated to the Christian concept of the "guardian angel" or "Holy Spirit," and its dangerous potentials were stripped away—banished, as it were, to the pagan wilderness, like scapegoats of Old Testament days. Not that the dangers ever really disappeared.

Early Christians, anxious to differentiate their "new," monotheistic religion from the preceding polytheistic "pagan" concepts, practices and traditions—at least the ones they could not pre-empt or absorb into their growing canon— reserved for the term *daimon* only its later, negative, "heretical" sense as an agent of the Devil. From this usage, we derive our modern term, *demon.*

Here is something Jung had to say about the *daimon:*

> The Greek words daimon and daimonion express a
> determining power which comes upon man from
> outside, like providence or fate, though the ethical
> decision is left to man. He must know, however,
> what he is deciding about and what he is doing.
> Then, if he obeys he is following not just his own
> opinion, and if he rejects he is destroying not just his
> own invention.[15]

As I compared my readings of Jung and others, with my dreams and waking experiences, I noticed that Jung used the phrase, *theriomorphic images of the Self.* "Theriomorphic" means "in the form of an animal"—especially in the sense of "animal images of divinity." To regard animals as manifestations of the divine is of course an ancient experience and practice among the earliest human cultures. That's undoubtedly why so many of the earliest *paleolithic cave paintings*, going back tens of thousands of years, depicted animals with such obvious devotion. Animal images predominated, humans less so. Sometimes in those ancient cave paintings, animals and humans were *fused* in what are often regarded as *shamanic* figures. After millennia, and well into the historical period, the animal images were still being combined with human figures, witness, for example, the many Egyptian deities combining animal and human attributes— hawk and human, crocodile and human, heron and human, hippo and human, snake and human. The natural world was sacred, as were the animals who, in evolutionary terms, all preceded humans, and usually by millions of years. Thus, the animals were intuitively understood as *ancestors*, as hosts and guardians of the spirit-world, i.e., the divine world to which the dead usually were thought to return.

It is interesting to me that, in those pre-Judeo-Christian cultures of ancient Egypt, Greece and Rome, representations of divinity often depicted a human figure *surmounted* by an animal face or head. The animal spirits form the "crown" or emblem *above* the human. Did the animal, to those venerable ancients, display the *higher* aspects of life on Earth, *above* the humans?

Even later Christian "angels," if you think about it, so essential to the monotheistic religion of a jealous God often portrayed as being utterly hostile to the priorities of the earlier pagan world, are regarded as carrying out "God's will." But is it really mere coincidence that angels are depicted as *animal-human* fusions—part-human, part-bird? I take that as a clear and obvious carryover from the earlier shamanic and pagan traditions.

The Heron Dreams

THIS MYTHOLOGICAL, RELIGIOUS AND HISTORICAL BACKGROUND may seem irrelevant to the story of Caborca and the herons, but it soon came to play a role in my dreams as the herons began to appear.

The first heron dream occurred within a year of my encounter with the heron on the beach that night on Puget Sound. It was a stunning dream, to be sure, but not in any way that made me want to crow like a rooster. On the contrary, it came to me like a slap in the face—which might have been the psyche's way of *keeping me from getting too inflated* with my secret discovery of dreams and herons and the *threads of destiny* they often reveal. Then again, at the same time the dream was illuminating, but in the painful way that an increase in consciousness often decrees. In that first heron dream:

> *I am at a city intersection. The traffic lights are red. Cars are lined up on the opposite side, waiting for the light to change. But in the middle of the intersection I see a tall heron, about six feet tall, in the middle of the pavement. The stationary cars rev their engines, impatient for the green light to appear, like race cars waiting for the checkered flag to start a race. I immediately see that the heron is in danger. I run into the intersection, knowing that if I don't reach it soon enough it will be run over by the cars. I run into the street and grab the enormous bird, hustling it off the street and onto a sidewalk—just in time! The cars rush off as I carry the bird down the sloping sidewalk away from the danger, hugging it to my face. I can feel the* realistic sensations of its feathers against my cheeks. *I whisper to this bird, "I love you." After carrying the heron down the block to the next cross-street, I set the heron down and it transforms into a blonde woman—a movie-star "blonde bombshell" type—who then gets into a pink Cadillac convertible and drives off.* [End of dream.]

I was both overjoyed and mortified. Overjoyed because a grand, six-foot-tall heron (over-life-sized!) had appeared in my dream. But why mortified?

First of all, my initial heron dream showed me that the magnificent bird—already a treasure of great value to me— was *in grave danger!* Otherwise, why were all the drivers gunning their engines while waiting for the light to turn green? And to do what? Only to run over the bird and rush off to their next superficial conquests! Had I not been eliminated from that very same "rat-race" mentality by the loss of my eye, I might have been right there among the other drivers, gunning my engine as well, oblivious to the presence of the heron, which probably would have been invisible to me in that case. Apparently, I was not yet far enough removed from the *soul-destroying complexes and attitudes of the culture and civilization that I grew up with.*

I felt a *deep, innate love* for the heron—or should I say, the "heron-woman"?—the implications of which are vast and complex. Somehow, I understood that the heron was a "soul-bird" for me. But the dream could not have stated more clearly the danger it was facing. Jung said, "The dream is its own interpretation." Intuitively, I added my own codicil to the dream's affidavit of self-revelation: If the heron was in danger, then I was in danger—in fact, my soul was in danger. That was a chastening realization.

And the transformation from *transcendent bird to human woman* told me that I was dealing with something alien to normal conscious awareness—yet capable of impinging upon that awareness. This phenomenon would obviously have repercussions for my experience of what Jung termed the *anima—the feminine aspect of a man's soul.* I was just beginning to learn about *anima projections,* and how much trouble they could stir up in a man's life—in *my* life! And the full magnitude of the task in its greater form was hinted at by Jung when he said, in so many words, that "the integration of the anima [into consciousness] is the *meisterstück* of psychological work."[16]

As I mulled over this dream[17]—it was obvious that the image of a "blonde bombshell driving off in a pink Cadillac convertible" was a terribly collective image, a pathetic cliché, projected onto human forms that are blown out of proportion thereby, because the human cannot contain divine energies without deformation. Was Marilyn Monroe, for example, really a "love goddess," a modern-day Aphrodite? She struggled to live a human life but was ultimately brought down in loneliness by the weight of collective projections—or so I suppose. That's the tragedy of so many "stars."

And that was part of the *warning* my first heron dream slipped into the slot of my *dream-letter-box*, like an engraved, cream-colored, hand-delivered envelope with fine, copperplate script, addressed to me. The perfumed letter inside the envelope began, *"My dear Paco"* . . .

But there was more. The finale to the dream—the blonde bombshell driving off in her pink Cadillac convertible—was like the punch line in a joke. But when I backed up from that point, rewinding the dream-reel by hand, frame-by-frame, the dream regained its serious portent, and the transformative, archetypal energy implicit in the *six-foot-tall heron that transformed into a woman,* showed me in clear and direct terms that I was the recipient of a ponderous, puzzling gift that it would take many years to unwrap, to discern and to respond to in some appropriate way.

As a final remark, I never before—to my knowledge—had had a dream in which the *sensate qualities of an imaginal figure* were so tremendously hyper-realistic, as when I carried the huge heron off the intersection and to safety. I could only conclude that this quality of the dream-image was telling me something about what I was dealing with—something far beyond my own personal, childhood complexes.

Something deep and mysterious, and greater than I. Something hyper-real.

The Heron Strikes . . .

65

TWO OR THREE YEARS PASSED BEFORE THE NEXT HERON DREAM occurred, and the transformative character of the dream-heron would assume even greater magnitude. Only this one was not a metaphorical "slap in the face" like the first. This one nearly snapped my head back. The occasion for this dream was a trip I was about to make to Pietrasanta, Italy, where I would be able to make sculpture in an Italian art-bronze foundry during a seven-week stint. I wanted to "incubate" a dream to carry with me to Italy—to request a dream, as it were, by focusing my attention every night before sleep, and then again every morning to see whether there had been a dream or not. One morning, a week or two before the trip, I awoke with a whopper.

In that dream:

> I am walking across a broad, grassy pasture—a place where animals are fed—with three or four other persons. We arrive at a cross-shaped intersection of fences, where gates are closely placed to facilitate changing the animals' grazing areas. I sense something approaching me from behind, and hear the flapping of wings. It is an enormous, six-foot-tall heron—well over life-sized. It circles around and lands in front of me, facing me. There is no doubt that the heron has come "for me." The bird's appearance is striking—it is bedraggled, fierce and desperate! As I look at it, it begins to shimmer and transform, from heron to human, back and forth. In its human form, it too is "bedraggled, fierce and desperate." A no-nonsense desperado, we might say. The great figure approaches me and, in its over-life-sized heron form, addresses me. It speaks to me in fluent Italian! I can understand what it is saying: It is demanding to be fed!
>
> Since I have forgotten the little Italian I learned in one college course I took fifteen years earlier, I answer in Spanish, saying to the heron: "No tengo

nada que darle." I don't have anything to give you.

   Whereupon the great bird strikes with its long, dagger-like beak, at my right eye! *Reflexively, I grab the thrusting beak in my hand, seeking to forestall grave injury, if not death. The bird is powerful, without doubt, but the dream ends in a stalemate: I have the heron's beak in my hand, but it takes all my strength not to be overwhelmed by the fierce bird-man and his demand to be fed.* [End of dream.]

Perhaps you can imagine how deeply this dream affected me. I had been captivated by herons since my encounter with the first one that night on the Puget Sound beach in the dark. In this dream, it was obvious that I was being confronted by a powerful, transcendent Being, part-bird/part-human, transforming back and forth, coming from *somewhere else,* and that it was making a demand on me—to *feed* him (her? it?). I would have to figure out how to do that. It was also obvious from the dream that the consequences for me, in the event of my failure to do so, would be severe. The image reminded me of the biblical story of Jacob *wrestling all night with the angel* at the ford, ending up in the morning with an injured hip.[18]

Often, we do not realize that the *details* in the mosaic-like imagery of a dream, or a dream series, however puzzling to our waking consciousness, are imbued with *necessity.* That is, they express something necessary, *the best way they can.* Thus, *the strike at my right eye,* not to mention the creature's strength, left no doubt about the dangers involved in denying the bird-man's demand. Perhaps the most shocking moment came sometime later, after I had transcribed my dream notes and pondered the dream-text and my associations to it many times over. That was the moment I realized with a shiver that the great heron-man had *not* struck at my left eye, *my seeing eye.* It had struck at my right eye, my missing eye, my prosthetic eye—my *"Caborca eye."*

67

In a flash of intuition I knew that this was a significant, symbolic detail of the dream, and the implications of that detail were massive and clear: *The heron was somehow implicated in the loss of my eye in Sonora, and it was pointing that out to me in the dream*. I could even imagine that the heron, because it was *symbolically implicated in the loss of the eye,* was also *symbolically present,* so to speak, during the accident, as if there had been some sort of presiding spirit *overseeing or guiding the event from above—or below—or within*. As if, let's say, the heron-guardian had "orchestrated" the event. Or something to that effect.

My vagueness here is both intentional and inevitable. It would be foolish to make too certain and positivistic a claim regarding what I do not really understand, *though I feel it intuitively and deeply*. But there was no doubt that I was up to my neck in mythic territory—however archaic or even preposterous we might regard such a position in today's *de-mythologized, de-sacralized* society. Mythic territory? Really? Yes, really.

In any event, the visual symbolism of the dream couldn't have been clearer in its implications. If the heron was symbolic, then Caborca too was symbolic; hence the loss of my eye was symbolic. In other words, the whole event and its aftermath could not be written off altogether as "merely accidental," which is what our present dominant, reductive view would claim. And if Caborca could not be written off and dismissed as merely accidental, then the whole *series* of experiences—from Caborca to herons to dreams to synchronicities—was also somehow *meaningful*. There was a *purpose* in it, however mysterious. The events were inter-related. But I did not yet know what that purpose and that meaning were. Why were they related? To find out more, I would have to keep dreaming.

The Blue Heron Foundry

MEANWHILE, HAVING BUILT MY OWN FINE-ART BRONZE FOUNDRY, and having made the trip to Italy, I was eagerly casting sculptures in bronze for regional artists and museums. As often as I could, I would cast my own work, including *bronze heron sculptures.* I had named the foundry the "Blue Heron Foundry." What else could it be? Whenever I received an invoice or receipt in the mail (no email in those pre-Internet days), I would look at the envelope, addressed to the "Blue Heron Foundry," and feel an *inward warmth or glow.* The folks at Federated Metals Division of ASARCO (American Smelting and Refining Company), who shipped me the pallets of bronze ingots that I used, couldn't have known that they, with their modern, high-tech, industrial capacities, were also facilitating my archaic, bronze-age, ritual celebration. Every time I melted a crucible of bronze, I burned a special Japanese incense. Superstitious? Very well if you insist. Call me superstitious. But to have neglected burning that incense would have amounted to *modern day hubris.*

Melting bronze to cast sculptures is an ancient process, possibly more than 7000 years old—the archeological discoveries of lost-wax metal castings keep pushing the age back in time. And, considering the intense temperatures involved in melting modern bronze alloys (to over 2000 degrees F.), and being subject to failures and mishaps, it lends itself to an archaic ritual attitude of devout preparedness. I was always aware of how old the tradition was that I was participating in. (Melting iron is a different process, with melting temperatures around 2800 degrees F., depending on the alloy. Hence, the Bronze Age was followed by the Iron Age, as iron demonstrated its superiority in tools and weaponry. Bronze Age warriors periodically had to *straighten* their swords during battle, and a well-wrought iron sword could cut through a bronze sword and be wrought to longer lengths as well—a definite advantage in close combat!)

About a year and a half after the second heron-dream of a six-foot-tall heron, this one striking at my Caborca eye and demanding to be fed, I had a third *heron dream,* which extended the motif portentously. In that dream:

Again, the dream takes place in a sweeping
grassy pasture—a place where animals are
often fed— but no fences or gates this time.
Instead, I see a group of wild horses running
together, right to left. I run after them for a
distance, until I come upon a dead heron
lying on the grass. That stops me in my
tracks, and at first I am shocked. But
suddenly I know what I have to do. I reach
down, take the beak in my hand, snap it off
and hold it in my hand. As the dream comes
to a close, I stand there in the grass, holding
the heron's beak in my hand, knowing that it
is a "special writing instrument." [End of
dream.]

Once again, I hold the dream-heron's beak in my hand, but this time I know what it will take to "feed the heron." Like it or not, *I will have to write.* So long as I make sincere efforts to fulfill that task, and knowing why, if not what, at least the dream-heron-daimon will not "starve" through my neglecting it.

When I had this dream, I was singlehandedly running the bronze foundry, remodeling my house top-to-bottom, still practicing and playing the flamenco guitar, transcribing and learning flamenco guitar solos from cassette tapes, giving guitar lessons and performing periodically, writing down my dreams, making sculpture, studying Jung, reading about ancient mythologies, walking the beaches, and so on.

When I woke up to the second *heron's-beak* dream, I knew that I had just been confronted with another major life-task— *to write*—just when I was already feeling overloaded. But there was no way I could refuse the dream.

So, I kept hammering and sawing wood, mixing plaster and melting bronze, transcribing and learning guitar solos, reading widely and recording dreams, all the while wondering to myself, "What the hell am I supposed to write?" And if my "special writing instrument" is a *heron's beak,* for God's sake, doesn't that suggest that my writing will have to be somehow

70

heron-like—i.e., sacred, sacerdotal, priestly or shamanic—since the heron-man dream figure was obviously evoking an archaic-yet-still-living god?

Some of the ancient Egyptian priests were known to use *ibis-beaks* for their stylus. Their god in that case was the Sacred Ibis of the Nile, so it made sense that their writing with an ibis-beak stylus must have been considered, in some sense, *sacred writing*. All their efforts were on behalf of the god. The god even owned the quarries from which the stones were mined that were then carved into likenesses of the god. And the very term *hieroglyphics* means "sacred carving or writing." I also knew that the ibis and heron were closely related in that antique religious mythology. Didn't I have to find some way of serving as a mouthpiece for the heron-man? A scribe? Bringing something to consciousness on his behalf? And the *heron-woman*, from the first dream, further increased the complexity of the situation. Quite beyond her implications for my personal *anima*-concerns, the heron-woman, when placed next to the heron man, implied some kind of *androgynous* or *hermaphroditic* quality or energy at an archetypal level. Two six-foot-tall herons: One transforms into a woman, the other transforms into a man! *"Mercurius duplex"* indeed! What next?

This second dream, in which I held the heron's beak again, had served up a daunting task. But, as is habitual with most dreams, it did so only in symbolic images that didn't *explain* anything so much as *hint at future potentials,* the way poems do. Though there were several more heron dreams in the series, the *"heron's beak"* dreams obviously formed a pair. In the second dream, *writing, and its deep engagement with language,* were made *explicit*, since the heron's beak was "a special writing instrument."

In the first dream, however, the language aspect was *implicit,* in one broad hint: the heron-man spoke to me in fluent Italian. *In fact, this mythological dream-figure seemed to possess far more Italian than I ever had before.* And since my classroom Italian had taken place fifteen years earlier, as I mentioned in the dream account, I only had a handful of Italian words left at my command at the time. I had forgotten most of it, because I hadn't been to Italy yet; had never had an occasion to use the Italian; had taken the course just out of *irrational exuberance*; etc. For years after the dream, I puzzled over this mystery: How did the heron-man learn to speak Italian with more fluency than I had ever attained myself in waking reality? I didn't think it was a matter of *cryptomnesia*—where you *remember* something in a dream that you've just *forgotten* in waking reality. Possible, maybe, but I didn't think so. Besides, it was a six-foot tall dream-heron that was doing the talking. Had that heron been looking over my shoulder fifteen years before, in my Italian class? Memorizing vocabulary lists, verb conjugations and different tenses along with me, as I studied the textbook? That didn't make sense.

One day, however, I registered a dawning realization, an intuition: The heron-man speaking Italian to me in a dream began to make sense if I regarded him/it as an archetypal, transpersonal *Spirit of Language*— or better yet, as an *Angel of Language*—coming to me with a message: *the demand to be fed*. The fact of his speaking Italian was symptomatic: in one sense, looking forward in time, personally, it anticipated my upcoming trip to Italy; but in another sense, perhaps archetypally, it referred me backward in time, linguistically, from Italian to Latin to Greek to Indo-European and perhaps even further back. Who knows how far?

To "communicate" with the heron-spirit and to feed it, would require incorporating new, spontaneous expressions of ancient truths of mythic depth. That's why Jung said, "The eternal verities cannot be passed on mechanically; rather, in every era, they must be born anew in the human soul."

Years later I happened to be reading two stunning works by the French Islamic scholar Henri Corbin, whose two principal books in English translation[19] dealt in depth with the works of the medieval Sufi mystic philosophers, Avicenna and Ibn Arabi. These Sufi masters belonged to a spiritual tradition that derived an entire cosmology from the actions of *angels*—an "angelology"—ranked in successive, concentrated but downward-tending tiers, until the divine impulse driving them splintered into the multitudinous human souls whom they activated and animated. Short of my having an equivalent experience—meditating to ecstatic heights on a "flying carpet"—this was still theoretical information to me. What really stunned me, however, was when I read this statement by Corbin, as if it had been written for me in answer to my questions: *"How do we feed the angel? We feed the angel with our substance."* Suddenly I had yet another hint to follow. I would have to feed the six-foot, Italian-speaking, transformative heron-man with my writing. What kind of writing? Well, first of all, it had to be substantial— *I had to write in order to feed the angel with my substance.* Secondly, it would in some way have to be *sacred.* Of course, it would be up to me to figure all that out—one word, one dream at a time.

Angel Power

AS IT TURNED OUT, I DIDN'T HAVE TO WAIT LONG for the next dream in the series. It was not a "heron dream," per se, but it stunned me nonetheless, and obviously it belonged to the whole Caborca-heron-daimon-angel leitmotif. In the dream:

> *I walk into a university classroom on the first day of class. The general subject is high-energy physics. This particular class is entitled "Angel Power." There are only two people in the room— myself and the "teacher," who happens to be a stocky, swarthy, dark-haired, powerfully-built Italian man! Not knowing what to expect, I am surprised when he walks up to me and immediately grasps my hand and engages me in an arm-wrestling test of strength.* [End of dream.]

As with the dream of the heron-man speaking Italian and striking at my Caborca eye, once again it took all my strength to hold my own against the Italian man's strength and power—his "Angel Power."

And once again, Henri Corbin's words—his *illuminations*—stepped into the fray, lending crucial assistance. I came across a comment he made about the biblical theme of "wrestling with the angel." According to Corbin, the motif of the "fight *with* the angel," is not a fight *against* the angel, it is actually a fight *for* the angel. And in a related insight, Corbin also said, "The angel's individuation comes first, then ours."

These two insights from Corbin turned my whole sense of the heron-angel dream-series around.

Instead of struggling defensively *against* the heron-man, or the "angel power" teacher, I had to consider the struggle as being *for them, a struggle on their behalf, that they should individuate first. Only thus could I individuate as well.* Their individuation came first. Fortunately, that was something I understood intuitively—even if dimly. I was not trying to *defeat* either figure, I was simply trying not to be destroyed by them. But now there was a difference. The purpose of the test of strength with the Italian-speaking heron-man and the Italian "angel power" teacher, was to *teach me,* in a sense, how much strength would be required to feed the angel. Namely, it would take *all my strength.* For, how could I possibly lend my efforts toward the individuation of a transcendent figure—*a daimon*—if my own strength were not somehow up to the task, if I could not match the angel's strength? That's why "feeding the angel" had to come from my "substance." In effect, I would be living my life on behalf of the angel, or the heron, or the heron-man. It would be that, or die.

The Heron Incubation

THE NEXT DREAM OF THE HERON-SERIES UPPED THE STAKES **yet** again, clarifying and confusing matters in one stroke:

Again, a heron flies up from behind and lands in front of me. And again, I know it has come "for me." This time I am standing next to a bench. Instinctively, I put my right foot on the bench to make a horizontal perch for the bird. It walks toward me, hops onto the bench, and from there hops onto my thigh. I can feel its claws grasping my leg, digging in. Then it hops up on my shoulders. Those claws again, digging in— not painful, exactly, but sharp, nonetheless. Then it hops on top of my head and nestles down. Once again, I feel the claws, now digging into my scalp! The sensations of claws and feathers on my body are quite distinct. As soon as the great bird is settled, I begin to feel heat building-up inside and around my head! And with the rising heat comes a golden radiance, emanating from my head. I can feel myself glowing! The heron remains nestled there, as if sitting on an egg. The culminating image, then, is that of a heron incubating my head, and golden radiance is the result! I open my arms in ecstasy, in what feels like a gesture of gratitude. [End of dream.]

Once again: If the dream is its own interpretation, in this case it seems straightforward. *The dream-heron incubates my dream-head, which then starts to glow.* That's the gist of it, but several things follow from that simple image.

We know that chicken eggs don't "glow" when they're being incubated by the hen that laid them. Rather, they get "warm." That's the point of the hen's incubation, as I found out in my neighbors' chicken-coop when I was five years old.

We also know that a *dream-heron* is not an empirical chicken; so, for a heron to incubate a human head in a dream, indicates that *two radically different orders of symbolic reality* are coming into play. In that case, the image of *incubating a human head,* as if it were an avian (or reptilian?) egg, might

75

suggest something along the lines of "protecting something in order for what is inside of it *to have time to grow.*"

Also, since it seems like folly to say that "the heron laid my head," the discrepancy between heron body and human head provides another *hint* about what this dream might be saying. I said above that *two radically different orders of reality* were coming together, not only meeting, but in some way conjoining, *as if they have come together, have "met" at the same level, and are forming a relationship that is capable of extending into consciousness—or at least meeting within the imaginal framework of a dream.*

Dreams do this all the time, like master chess players that are way ahead of the dreamer, setting up situations where all kinds of repercussions will follow.

In this case, the dreaming ego is being protected by the dream-heron—presumably, *the daimon*— which suggests that *a relationship in fact already exists between the two,* between the ego-personality and the transpersonal emissary from the objective psyche. But how conscious is the relationship? Frankly, I'm learning as I go! I notice that the transpersonal figure *comes to* the ego-personality, and not vice versa, recalling Henri Corbin's declaration that, "It is for them [the angels] to come to us."

Sequence of Dreams, Trail of Hints

IT IS PROBABLY NO ACCIDENT THAT PALEOLITHIC HUNTERS, weavers of fairy tales, let alone whoever weaves our dream narratives, are all familiar with the motif of leaving *a trail of hints*—like crumbs of bread, or seeds, that lead somewhere. In the case of stone-age hunters, the trail may lead right into a spring-rigged snare. In a fairy tale, Hansel left a trail of breadcrumbs in the forest so that he and Gretel could find their way back out. Likewise, the ball of thread that Ariadne gave to Theseus to help him out of the Minotaur's labyrinth. And so forth. Whether leading-in or leading-out, the trail of hints is an archetypal motif.

In the case of our dreams, it is likely that those who keep track of their own dreams for any length of time will find trails of hints—motifs—that lead them deeper into the psyche. We could say that every dream in itself is a hint of something that leads the dreamer "forward," in once sense or another, to the next hint, even when it seems to lead "backwards." As the French say, *"Reculer pour mieux sauter!"* One step backward, the better to leap forward!

Nor would I say that every "trail" is a safe one or should inevitably be followed. So much depends on the dreamers, the degree of comfort and familiarity they have with the irrational symbolisms of dreams, and perhaps what is at stake. To quote Jung again, in an excerpt-from-the-excerpt included above:

> No one should deny the danger of the
> descent, but it can be risked. No one need
> risk it, but it is certain that someone will.
> And let those who go down the sunset way
> do so with open eyes, for it is a sacrifice
> which daunts even the gods.

Hence, the warnings implicit in the dreams: As my two dreams clearly indicated—where the six-foot heron struck at my "Caborca eye," and where the "Angel Power" teacher arm-wrestled me in a test of strength—to follow the trails presented by dreams may at the very least require considerable courage and strength, and a willingness to undergo unknown risks.

Oftentimes, the other side of a warning is a promise. The later dream—of the heron incubating my glowing head—is like *the promise of a gift*—surely a wonderful thing, especially when received and enacted in some appropriate way by the ego associated with that "head." But what about the gift that is delivered to the ego from the psychic depths in an extraordinary dream, but *the gift is ignored or disparaged, left undeveloped, the responsibility refused*? If that happens often enough, then there is a chance the gift will turn against us. There is a saying attributed to Jesus in the Gnostic Gospel of

Thomas, found in Nag Hammadi, Egypt, in 1945, that puts a sharp point on this common danger:

> Jesus said: If you bring forth what is within
> you, what you bring forth will save you. If you
> do not bring forth what is within you, what you
> do not bring forth will destroy you.

Such a deep psychological insight, from the antique days before there was anything called "psychology." It would serve as a clear warning in any age. The saying is probably at least 2000 years old, but I suspect it was already a venerable insight when the first scribe wrote it down. And even if it was a revolutionary, unheard-of advance when it was written, it still is resonant with nature's own deep wisdom, to my ear at least. In fact, I am sorely tempted to apply that gnostic saying to humanity as a whole. Over evolutionary stretches of time, we have received tremendous gifts from the gods, or from nature, or from God, or from whatever *donor* we care to envision and give a name to. Yet I can't help but feel that in recent centuries we have been squandering our birthright by our widespread refusal of dreams, which come to us from our deepest reaches. Instead of bringing forth the inherent, divine gifts, we prefer to appropriate the divine powers ourselves altogether, to "play God," serving the ego instead of the Other. How much of the destructiveness that is so prevalent today comes about because of our refusal of the implications of that gnostic saying?

Here is another interesting aspect of the incubation dream, and it's pretty simple. If whatever was being incubated were eventually to "hatch," something might emerge that could eventually "fly." My conjecture here is that the incubating heron implies that "spiritual" contents or insights were being cultivated for eventual release and development.[20] I am all too aware of the dangers of inflation when confronted with archetypal dream images like these, so I don't want to get caught up in grandiose assumptions—especially when dealing with a series of heron dreams that takes me, through various pathways, back to Egyptian creation myths about the *bennu bird,* the *"fire-bird"* and the beginning of the World of Time at the moment of the Primordial Sunrise.

On the other hand, the whole series is so compelling to me, that I don't dare discount its importance and value out of fear of "inflation"—which term, as used in economics, implies a lessening of inherent or intrinsic value, like Roman coins that over centuries were cheapened by reducing the gold or silver content while maintaining the same old "face value."

In archaic, shamanic times, there would have been no doubt about the heron-incubation dream: the daimon was communicating with me and it would be my "shamanic" responsibility to incorporate its messages into my life and, as required and so far as possible, to convey those messages to my "tribe."

For any modern individual, however, all of those archaic pathways have to be reinvented, *invested with new meanings.* But I knew I couldn't fulfill my "shamanic responsibility," if we dare call it that, by submerging my individuality through identity with a *group.* My individuality would have to come from more authentic—more individual—means and sources, though someday I might be able, through individual efforts, to *serve* some larger group.

Symbols and the Symbolic

THE WORD "SYMBOL" DERIVES FROM THE GREEK, *SUN-,* *"with, together,"* + *ballein,* "to throw" (cf. the modern English term, "ballistics"). The general sense is "to throw together." Thus symbols—unlike signs, which designate something known—always throw together two or more elements, something *known* and something *unknown.* That's probably why dreams can never be exhausted, never drained, never fully understood or interpreted, no matter how many explanations or interpretations we might wish to bring to bear upon them.

Take for example the word *heron.* Understood in its function as a *sign,* the word refers to the empirical, widely dispersed wading bird of an ornithological category, a specimen of the species *Ardea Herodias Linneaus,* family *Ardeidae,* and so on.

But, understood in its function as a symbolic image, *"heron"* throws the long-legged wading bird, together with (1) Dylan Thomas's poetic *"heron-priested shore";* and (2) the sacred Egyptian *bennu bird,* depicted as a heron, who called out the moment of creation on the First Day of the world, when the primordial Nile floodwaters began to subside and the Primal Mound first appeared in the shape of a pyramid with a smaller, pyramid-shaped "cap" fashioned out of gold, to crown the top, the gold representing the rays of the rising sun on that primordial First Day of Creation; and (3) the heron-headed manifestation of Ra, the Egyptian sun-god, perched in the bow of the solar barque as it arrives at *sunrise* to renew the world with each new day, after its passage through death and the underworld darkness of the night; and (4) the Greek *boinu*— derived from Egyptian *bennu*—and the Latin *phoenix,* derived from Greek *boinu,* all representations of the mythical bird that lives 500 years, dies, bursts into flames, and is re-born out of its own ashes, hence the *mythological principle of self-renewal, of death and re-birth.* And so forth.

The heron-bennu-boinu-phoenix complex is the prototype of the various cultural manifestations of the mythical *firebird.* All symbolic, yet also *implicit* in the everyday heron that raids your backyard pond for its fish and frogs. And I confess that there have been certain times when I felt, intuitively, that the empirical heron I encountered in a synchronistic experience while awake, was *the same heron* that the Egyptians recognized as a manifestation of the divine—a god. Don't worry. I know how "crazy" this sounds, but so many of my experiences have far exceeded the bounds of "rationality" that, at this point, *cela m'est égal.* In short, I don't care if it sounds crazy.

With symbols, then, the list just goes on and on. Thus, the image—"heron"—especially a six-foot-tall heron-man that speaks fluent Italian in a dream—*that* heron can never be pinned down, or reduced to *nothing but* gristle and bone, gut and feather, i.e., *nothing but materiality without meaning.* It is a symbol. One manifestation of an archetype.

The various qualities of the *heron-as-symbol* would be obvious enough if one only *read in history books* about the mythical attributes of the heron. But for me, its appearances in my dreams and synchronistic experiences in waking life, walking the beaches, or before my lunar eye, had the effect of verifying its mythical presence as *a living force both in my outer life and my deepest interiority*.

The Heron Sunrise

ONE MORNING I AWOKE AT 5:30 AM. I'd had a compelling dream during the night and had scribbled some dream-notes on the pad by my bed. The notes were terse, as usual, but also easier to read than usual. I was excited. The notes read:

> *Drive to local beach. Low tide. Water-birds—*
> *many sea-gulls—work tide-flat for food. I scan*
> *area, look for heron. See* two herons *among*
> *other birds. Unusual! Never saw two before. One*
> *heron picks up crab in beak, swallows it whole.*
> *Didn't know herons could eat crabs!* [End of dream.]

I practically flew out of bed, got dressed and drove downtown to my "dream-restaurant," where it was my custom to transcribe my dreams every morning into a permanent, hardbound dream-book. As soon as I reached the main street, I looked at the water. It was low tide, as in my dream, and the sun had not risen yet. At that moment, I knew intuitively that I would see a heron that morning, even though I hadn't seen one for *two months*! Today, my luck would change, I felt certain. The restaurant opened at six. I would get there just in time. I couldn't wait to transcribe the dream.

It was a beautiful morning. To the west, it was still night, and the sky was a deep indigo blue, sparkling with tiny stars. To the east, the Cascade Mountains in the distance were becoming visible in silhouette, illuminated from behind by the shifting curtain of those pastel colors streaming upward from the approaching, not-yet-risen sun. The air was still. The shadowed water was glassy calm. The world seemed to be suspended, on pause, holding its breath, all in abeyance.

As I pulled into the restaurant parking lot, I glanced out toward the bay and immediately saw a heron, wading along the edge of the shore. The bird was perhaps twenty or thirty yards away, but I didn't want to disturb it. So, I drifted to a stop, quietly latched the door of my truck, carried my dream-book inside and found a table with a view of the entire bay.

I verified the position of the heron and determined that it was in no hurry at all. It was taking its time, again, the way herons do. I opened my dream book, took out my pen, and began to write down the dream.

Meanwhile the heron meandered, stopping occasionally to preen its feathers, or to spear some unfortunate creature at its feet—or was the creature fortunate, to be assimilated into a heron?

The colors from behind the mountains changed their pastel hues, intensifying as the hidden sun advanced. The heron continued walking, stopping, walking, preening, stopping again. Patient.

I finished transcribing the dream and began writing a description of the event I was witnessing. In my own heron-like fashion, I wrote, pausing occasionally to watch the heron, wrote some more, watched again. I knew this was a momentous day.

Then suddenly the moment had arrived. As the blazing disk of the sun finally edged above the distant horizon, the heron had reached a point that was exactly, geometrically, in a direct line between me and the rising sun. The glassy water, undulating gently in the background, began to sparkle with tiny golden bursts of sunlight. As I squinted in the brightness, the blurred sparks enlarged to form golden circles on the water, like quivering doubloons, rising and falling.

Then, as the first rays of the sun came streaking across the water, the heron was backlighted, outlined with gold, as if its entire body were emitting a nimbus and had begun to blaze.

Then it shook its beak, and drops of golden water, flung to each side, spilled into the water at its feet.

The hair stood up on the back of my neck, and I heard a word, as if spoken by an autonomous Voice, which simply said: "Egypt."

I felt myself go into a kind of eclipse, like a form of timelessness. I felt a dissolution of boundaries as I was "taken up" into the moment—the sun, the heron, the mountains, the water, the wiggling fish, the yellow beak, the sparkling doubloons, the dream, the Voice, the word, the implications beyond words. I don't know how long that effect lasted, but I know that, metaphorically, I was *on fire* for the duration. Maybe that's how Bernini's Santa Teresa felt in her ecstasy when the angel speared her heart, filling her with divine love.

Eventually, the sun cleared the mountains and climbed higher. The pastel colors yielded to the brightness of daylight. The heron continued walking, as I continued writing. The waitress brought more coffee, but I wanted to shout: "But don't you see? I don't need any coffee. My cup runneth over!" But I didn't say that. I only murmured politely, "Thank you."

I can't be sure, but I suspect I was the only person in the restaurant that morning who witnessed the great, cosmic, mythological event, the only person who had been set on fire by an epiphany of the sun-god and its emissary, the fire-bird.

There was no way I could have "shared" the moment of the heron-sunrise and the dream, with the men who came there every morning for coffee and dice, before going to work at the tire shop next door. I had just had a religious experience, but I was bound to become more isolated than ever. For, as Jung once said:

> Religious experience is absolute. It is indisputable. You can only say that you have never had such an experience, and your opponent will say, 'Sorry, I have.' And there your discussion will come to an end.

It is a sad fact of our time that experiences such as I just recounted, are generally overlooked, ignored, disparaged or kept secret—though I think they are *more common than we realize*. The worldview that predominates in this secular age of ours does not, as a rule, look kindly on private religious experiences—the ones that take place *extra ecclesiam*, "outside the church," beyond the boundaries of orthodoxy and convention. We seem to have such a horror of appearing different, of becoming who we actually are in the deepest sense, of becoming individuals, and standing forth as such, that our most authentic qualities, and the experiences that reveal those qualities, tend to get suppressed. Who knows how much illness today results from those suppressions, or repressions, of our inner truths? What price should we expect to pay for living a virtual lie? As one of my favorite flamenco *letras* puts it: *"Pa' qué quieres más castigo que vivir sin conocerte?"* Why should you want any greater punishment than to live without knowing yourself?

I have said it many times in different ways, but it is my contention in this volume that *the loss of my eye in that bizarre accident in Mexico was part of the price being extracted from me by transcendent forces that had some other purpose in mind than my just following the crowd.* To become the person that I most authentically am, with all the good and bad that entails, is one way of imagining what this series of dreams was demanding of me—as my way of "feeding the angel." The point could be argued until doomsday, of course, but to say that there was a great *demand being placed on me,* seeded throughout many dreams, is beyond doubt. I have only recounted a few of the dreams here.

We can see what I called "the horror of appearing different," of standing firm as an individual, being reflected to us today in what seems like a perverted or distorted form. For, increasingly, we mistake our true *individuality* for mere *individualism*. Individualism, with its fast-mutating, trendy, outward displays, shows exaggerated symptoms of anxious narcissism, like a mass regression to tribalistic belonging— outrageous hairdos, mandatory tribal tattoos, ubiquitous piercings, outlandish clothes, incessant social media posts, the virtual Noah's-flood of thumbnail photographs of ourselves—

an infinitude of "selfies"—flashing around the world in mini-seconds, by the millions—maybe even billions. Entertaining? Yes, apparently. But deeply satisfying? Hmmmm.

I wonder: Are we really so inwardly uncertain that we constantly have to put ourselves on display, as if always fishing for compliments? What happens to the authentic inner person in all this anxiety and outward display? This is an *introvert* speaking, of course. But to me, these otherwise superficial phenomena appear to be symptomatic of the deeper spiritual crisis of our age. The suffering in the world is titanic and growing only worse. Floodwaters rise above our ankles. Wildfires overtake us as we run. The air rankles in our lungs. Koalas cry out as they burn. Pandemics sweep the globe. While we…

I make no claim that what I say here will make *any difference at all* in the larger trends I just pointed to. I simply offer my dreams and experiences, the way *pre-electrified* farmers offered up cups of water to *prime* their hand-pumps, to bring more water up from their wells. The priming of a water-well works through the *surface-tension of water molecules.* I think there is a kind of *surface-tension of dream-water*, the psychic substance *par excellence.* For example, hearing someone else's dream can bring one's own dream to the surface, into the light. And then there may be psychic movement, as when dream-water touches dream-water.

So many memories are locked away in strongboxes, so many dreams discarded on dung-heaps, so many angels appear in dreams, only to be pushed away unfed. I was fortunate, to have been slapped silly, slapped awake. To an extent, my deepest experiences have indeed isolated me, but I know for a fact that *I am not alone in having them.* People all over the world are working on them.

My guess is that all but the most *guarded* and *armored* of people have had their own memorable moments of epiphany—synchronicities in which they too felt their meaningful connectedness to the great forces of the universe, like I did. I would be especially happy if my words here were to evoke memories of unusual moments during *childhood* for any reader, before the regimented training of schools and *de-*

sanctified work has alienated them from themselves; but I would also—if I could—evoke in any reader their own moments of crisis, or of near-death, like Caborca was for me, or even just moments of quietness, of doing nothing, with no particular anxious intention, when the whispering voices of what we used to call "angels and epiphanies" can still be heard.

Speaking of which, my account of the "heron-sunrise" is not finished. As if what I had already witnessed from inside the café at the moment of the sunrise was not enough, I went outside and climbed a small hill—a big pile of leftover glacial sand that had not been bulldozed away when the restaurant and its parking lot were built.

I scrambled up the hill, sat down and watched the heron, which by this time had meandered about *a quarter mile farther down the beach*. At which point a *second heron* flew up to it from across the water, landing next to it on the beach. Despite the distance between me and them, I could see them performing the ritual heron-courtesies before continuing together their hunt for food.

The fact that now there were *two herons*, as in my dream that very morning, when I had, in my entire life, only seen *one heron at a time*, reinforced the feeling I had about that sunrise moment—the feeling that I was in the presence of some great, transpersonal force. Jung named the phenomenon of meaningful coincidence, "synchronicity." This takes place when two events coincide in time, but with a felt and perceived *meaning* that connects them, a meaning too powerful to be denied but that cannot be explained or rationalized away by causality. When the "coincidence" is just too powerful in its significance, and the chances against its ever happening are a million-to one—then maybe something important is taking place. Jung sub-titled his hypothesis of synchronicity, "*an acausal connecting principle*." Causality is our grand explanatory principle. But it cannot "explain" every single event.

After I had sat on the glacial mound for twenty minutes or so, watching the herons far away down the beach, they both leaped into the air at once, pumping their great wings in that slow wing-beat that is so close in tempo to my fairly slow heart-beat. They flew diagonally across the angle of my vision, obviously on their way to an island across the bay, where I assumed, they had either a nest—my guess—or at least a roosting spot.

When they were about half-way out across the water, however—a matter of more than a mile—one of the herons peeled away from its mate, and *flew straight back to where I was sitting.* It landed on the rocky beach *directly below where I sat,* and it stood in that one spot for about ten minutes. Why did it leave its partner and fly back, from *half-way across the bay,* to where I sat? Did the heron know I was aflame? Did *I* have a radiant nimbus? Was this another message from the *angelos,* Greek for "messenger"? What do herons know and when do they know it? I couldn't answer the questions, of course, but I would sit there as long as the heron stayed.

Finally, it leaped up again, flew out over the water and disappeared across the bay, to join its mate.

That synchronistic event is one of the most powerful experiences of my life—powerful in its emotional impact and deep significance. Another one-in-a-million chance against it happening at all. Yet it did happen, and it was part of the chain of dreams and experiences that connect back in time to Caborca, and, I continue to imagine, "forward" in time, somehow, to my final fate and my death. Like a cybernetic feedback loop of shared, profound meaning.

My first and foremost task was to *respond to the heron dreams* by accepting the ethical challenge they all presented, and incorporating them and their messages, somehow, into my life. Dream figures bring us their hints, cast in the primordial language of symbolic images, and our task is *to realize the creative potentials implicit in both dreams and dream figures, symbols and images,* and to do so within our empirical, waking lives, *however we can.* This belongs somehow to the phenomenology of *incarnation.*

During those heron years, I frequently read the great Welsh poet Dylan Thomas, having committed several of his poems to memory. One particular poem, "Poem on His Birthday," contained several lines that buzzed me like live electrical wires, resonating strongly with my own beach-and-river experiences of the priestly, holy herons as they performed their daily sacraments. Thomas wrote that poem on his 35th birthday, hence the title. And, like the call-and-response of a cathedral liturgy, he finishes each of the first three dream-like stanzas with a sacred heron image:

> Herons spire and spear. Herons, steeple-stilted, bless. Herons walk in their shroud..."

And, finally, in the middle of the ninth stanza he writes:

> Oh, let me midlife mourn by the shrined /And druid herons' vows/The voyage to ruin I must run...

The shrined and druid herons' vows! Oh my! It is clear to me that Dylan Thomas was a mystic, a nature-poet, a great Welsh bard of the grand and ancient oral tradition, and he obviously had strong feelings and intuitions about the herons and all the other creatures who plied their eternal trades in and around the waterways of Wales. In a sense, Dylan Thomas and his poetry guided me as I went about finding *my* trades, picking up the pieces of my shattered life. By degrees, it dawned on me that the world was enchanted and ensouled, and I was in thrall to it.

Cow Skull Burial

THERE IS A HIDDEN DYNAMIC TO OUR ACTIONS, INTENTIONS and reflections, that does not find much of a purchase in this extraverted, technological, scientific, biblical, patriarchal, atheistic, money-and-power-obsessed, military, corporate, consumer society. Usually we make decisions and take actions according to our assessments of their utility or advantages to us in the social, political or economic fields to which we belong. Even in our good deeds for others, there often lurks a self-conscious, inwardly-mirrored, narcissistic appraisal of *how noble we are.* I personally think that this American trait derives, *at least,* from as far back as the Puritan colonists in New England, a period when outward displays of personal *piety* were expected and valued—for example, piously reading the Bible aloud to the family around the table at night after dinner—more valued by Puritans and many Protestants than participation in traditional Catholic sacraments (which Protestants have often called "popery"). The expression "holier than thou" may give voice to this pietistic, moralistic, puritanical inclination.

When I speak of a *hidden dynamic,* I am talking about something closer in spirit to private prayer or individual ethical values than to the *outward display of public piety.* But taking a moral or ethical action because of an obligation to a *dream,* or to an *animal,* or to the command of an authoritative *inner Voice,* can have surprising effects that don't generally attach to the orthodox actions of individuals in response to group expectations.

The actions I want to highlight here are by and large *invisible.* They do not register on the collective radar screen. This hidden dynamic can be found in the unanticipated synchronistic consequences that seem to be "attracted" to certain actions. I learned this one unusual night during my years living in the "heron- priested" waters of Puget Sound.

One day a friend stopped by my house unannounced, and, with no explanation, gave me a sun-bleached cow skull he had found somewhere. Not inclined to look a gift horse in the mouth, I accepted the white skull and set it on a patio deck. Naturally I thought immediately about the cow in Caborca, but no bells rang, and I soon forgot about it. For several weeks I moved it occasionally, not quite finding the right spot for it.

At the time, I was working on expanding my scant memories of the eye-accident, which at this point had taken place around twenty years earlier. Looking at my scattered notes and documents, it suddenly occurred to me that I had gone through that entire traumatic episode and its aftermath, without formally acknowledging the death of the cow that had been the instrument of my transformation—the *causa efficiens,* as the philosophers say. The cow had died unnoticed, uncelebrated, unthanked. Nothing had been spoken, nothing voiced, no story proclaimed, no eulogy intoned. Nothing. The cow had just vanished in a frantic peal of shrieking rubber on pavement, and a blast of black metallic lacerations under a slice of the dying moon.

Had that cow not been standing in that road that night, blocking Phil's and my forward progress, presenting its black flanks to our speeding VW—an unconscious presentation, to be sure—then perhaps I would not have lost my eye. But by the same token, I might not have received the gift of *awakening,* for that's what the accident was—a "wake-up call."

Realizing my lapse, I undertook to make a restitution. I would honor the cow that had been so important to me, by enacting some kind of ritual gesture. Then I remembered the white cow skull that had been drifting around, "looking for a place to land."

That cow skull was the obvious object around which to build the ritual. I decided I would bury it at a certain place on the heron-sunrise beach, where, in the late-nineteenth century, it was rumored that a slaughterhouse had stood on now-rotted pilings that extended out into the water. According to the ecology of the times, the carcasses of cattle and sheep were dumped off the end of the pier, food for crabs and fish. Out-of-sight, out-of-mind was the ecological thinking, I assumed.

I knew from my morning strolls on the heron-sunrise beach, next to the dream-restaurant, that the rumors of the slaughterhouse were true. As proof, I often found cows' and sheep's teeth (incisors and molars), and jawbones of both kinds, with and without the teeth intact, washed up on the beach after storms. But you had to have a keen eye to spot those things. They were easily mistaken for half-buried rocks or broken shells, often barely protruding from the wave-lapped sand. But I had a keen eye derived from my heron-spotting, and I found a lot of them.

From early on I referred to that beach as "the Tooth Beach." And since it was obviously also the "Place of the Dead

Cows," it was therefore the only place where I felt justified in carrying out my ceremony. The ritual would take the only fitting form: a *burial of the cow skull*, with some kind of eulogy intoned over it. But the skull had to be buried *under water*, because that's where all the other dead cows and their bodily detritus lay. (Dylan Thomas would have understood that.) Besides, I didn't want anyone happening upon it and digging it up as some profaned trophy, the way British archeologists robbed Egyptian royal tombs.

Obviously, then, the skull had to be buried at the *deepest low tide, as close to the anniversary of the accident as possible*. I found a tide-table booklet and checked the dates and depths. On the date I selected, the low-tide would reach its maximum at around 1:00 AM in the morning, which happened to be the approximate time of the cow-eye-accident as well. So, it was settled.

The day of the event, I took a magic marker with waterproof-ink and wrote on the broad forehead of the white skull:

"To the Cow That Died, September 10, 1963." Then I signed it. "Paco Mitchell."

From my foundry I took a burlap sack (which was handy for cutting into strips to use as reinforcement for plaster molds), some black rubber boots, a flashlight and a spade-shovel. Placing the inscribed skull in the rough cloth sack, I put my "ritual kit" in the back of my red pickup truck. I was ready. It occurred to me, of course, that no church congregation within a radius of several thousand miles would have any inkling that what I was doing had anything to do with a "religious impulse." Voodoo maybe, or perhaps a Christian rattlesnake-ecstasy cult in the Deep South, but certainly no self-respecting proper Christian would smile on me. No purple-velveted, silver-chaliced, carved and oaken altar would have been made available to me. My sacramental ritual offering would be carried out with burlap, a shovel, wet sand, wind and rocks— or nothing at all.

It only remained for the hour of departure to arrive. I had set the alarm and gone to bed early, to get some rest from working all day at the foundry. The bell rang, or the buzzer

91

buzzed, and I got out of bed, dressed in warm clothes and went out to the truck. It was an old Ford F-250 three-quarter-ton pickup with a 360ci V8 engine. I called it the "Red Gorilla." The big engine kicked over and caught, rumbling in the dark. Slipping it into gear, I eased the clutch and set forth slowly and solemnly, my ritual kit in the back.

I lived in a small town, so there was never any traffic at this hour of the night, and any one point was separated from any other point by about a five-minute drive or so. Soon I had reached the waterfront drive, the main street of downtown. Still no traffic. The only car in evidence, in fact, was the blue patrol car in front of the local police department. The light inside the police station was on. Maybe the patrolman was catching up on paperwork. Maybe he had night duty. Maybe he had handcuffed some malefactor and was booking him. Rumbling past the patrol car, I practically idled through the few commercial blocks of the Victorian town, which I think of as "a china cup by the sea." Very pretty.

But my thoughts tonight were not on ornate architecture, or four-masted 19th-century lumber schooners anchored in the bay or hand-carved corbels. The closer I got to the Tooth Beach, the more focused
I became, and my thoughts orbited like planets around the ritual I had planned and was about to perform. Truthfully, I hadn't planned very much. I was winging it. As for the eulogy I would recite, my "plan" was to say whatever came into my mind.

Then I arrived at the restaurant, turned into the parking lot and killed the engine.

I confess that I was slightly concerned about that blue patrol car, because it was almost one o'clock in the morning. The restaurant was closed. The private parking lot was empty. All of downtown was empty, except for the cop and me. If the patrolman had to go somewhere in a hurry—or even just roll in a leisurely manner down the main street as I had—maybe he would notice my truck in the parking lot under the bright lights. Wouldn't that be suspicious to the law-enforcement imagination, the one that tends to imagine crime wherever it looks? A beat-up red Ford anachronism sitting all by itself in the vacant parking lot? Under the blazing security lights? At one AM?

How would I explain myself should he happen to stop to check out the truck? "What was that, officer? Me? What am I doing here?"

"Well, you see, I'm just going to perform a little religious ritual out on the beach here. It won't take very long."

"What's that? No, sir, I'm afraid it can't wait until morning. You see, I have to bury this old cow skull out on the beach at the lowest possible tide."

"Where's the skull? Well, it's in this old burlap bag, of course. Here it is. It's a beauty, isn't it?" "No, officer, *I don't go around all the time collecting dead skulls to bury.* Just this one time, and this skull is *special.* And look here! This is the shovel I'm going to use to dig the hole for the burial. The handle's starting to crack, but the shovel still has a lot of life left in it, don't you think?"

"No, officer, I'm afraid I don't belong to a Satanic cult. No cult at all. In fact, no church at all. I'm making this up as I go."

"Lawyer? No, I don't have a lawyer, let alone a good one. Tell it to the judge? What judge? You're kidding. Isn't he the one they call the 'Hanging Judge'?"

Needless to say, the patrolman never showed up and I never had to give an explanation, but still I was nervous, because it felt like I was committing a crime, violating the bounds of legal, acceptable behavior. But this was a necessary action I was taking, and the judgment would eventually be delivered in a higher—or perhaps a lower—court.

I took the burlap sack with its skull, the flashlight and the shovel, put on the rubber boots, and slid down the embankment to the heavy stones that served as a breakwater—to keep strong waves from washing away the restaurant. There was not much sand on the exposed beach here. Rocks of different sizes, strands of kelp and seagrass, an old tire or two. The sky was dark and overcast. No moon, the same as in Caborca the night of the accident. I went as far out as the water permitted—it was low tide indeed—and selected a spot between some rocks. My first attempts to dig were thwarted by buried rocks. I changed locations and had slightly better luck. I managed to excavate enough of a hole to bury the skull completely. I covered it with rocks, because I didn't want nosy scuba-divers or snorkelers poking around my sacred burial ground.

So. Everything was ready. Time to deliver my speech.

I waited for my thoughts to clear. I didn't even know whom to address. The cow? Phil? My mother? The herons?

Finally, I just lifted my arms skyward and whispered, as fervently as I could, "Thank you."

A few tears rolled, but I knew that whatever I was involved in was way over my head, was vastly bigger than I was, bigger than my life, bigger than my potentials, let alone my faults. I suppose I was really addressing *the intelligence of the universe*, offering gratitude for *the fact of my existence*, any existence at all, in fact, grateful to be alive on this planet, on this beach, at this hour, standing in rubber boots with a flashlight and shovel in my hands amidst the sporadically spitting clams.

When I had finished with the ritual, I gathered everything and walked back toward my truck, past the old tires and the spitting clams, buried in their snug little sandcastles. I scrambled back up the embankment, loaded my gear in back of the truck and got into the cab. The engine fired right up, and I rumbled out of the parking lot and back down the main drag. Rumbling is what that truck mostly did. The blue patrol car was gone.

I came to an intersection and was about to turn and drive over the hill to home and to bed, like any sensible person. But I hesitated. I was feeling something, like a restraint. As I released the clutch and began moving slowly forward, the truck's steering wheel turned back toward the beach. Something had apparently decided that I was not going home yet after all, as if there still remained some unfinished business. *That something had decided that I was going back to the beach.* But this time it was not the Tooth Beach where I was headed. I was going to park in front of the police station and walk across the street to a small public park directly across the street. Since it was a public park, *not a private parking lot,* I wasn't concerned about questions I might not have to answer. Besides, I wouldn't be carrying a burlap sack with a cow skull inside, or a shovel and flashlight, or wearing rubber boots. I would be just a normal, law-abiding, average citizen (well, almost), spending a little time in the public beach, in the dark, at the water's edge, between one and two o'clock in the morning. Easy to explain: "Just a mild case of insomnia, officer, you know what I mean? Do you ever get insomnia?"

I walked straight toward the water and sat on one of the park benches, which was placed next to a public pier and looked out over the water, which I could have seen in the daytime. Tonight, of course, it was too dark. When I looked out on the bay, I couldn't see a thing. To my left, down the beach a hundred yards or so, I could see a tugboat and a fuel barge, off-loading heating oil or gasoline to some storage tanks. The sound of the diesel pumps was audible, and a bright floodlight on the tug illuminated all the pipes, valves and gauges. Fortunately, the floodlight was directed away from me. I turned away from the glinting light and just wanted to feel the dark presence of the gentle, lapping water in front of me.

Then I noticed a faint luminosity moving in the darkness ahead. I couldn't tell what it was, but it was definitely faintly luminous, and vertical as well. Even more bizarre, it looked like it was *dancing* at the edge of the water. It was at the very threshold of visibility and therefore something liminal (*limen* = Latin for "threshold"). A vertical, dancing phenomenon, now visible, now invisible. Actually, it looked like a *luminous, dancing, vertical snake,* a shining sinuousity in motion, dancing and darting in the dark, a fluid scripture of serpentine hieroglyphics in the cold night air.

I was mesmerized, but I truly did not know what I was seeing. I watched for several minutes, never having witnessed anything remotely similar to it.

Then, with a shiver of intuitive recognition, *at last I realized what it was*. I was seeing the throat, neck and breast plumes of a Great Blue Heron, moving against the utterly dark background. The feathers were reflecting the dim light from the mercury-vapor lamp perhaps seventy or eighty yards behind me, in front of the police station. Once I realized what it was, my mind could fill in the blanks and I could better discern the form and shape, the angles and movements of the heron's gesticulating body. I had spent so many hours watching them, I felt like I knew their movements by heart. Now here I was, well past one o'clock in the morning, sitting on a bench in total darkness, having just come from burying the cow skull at low tide, to honor the cow that died in Caborca, watching a heron move back and forth at the edge of the water.

Furthermore, I could now see that it was *fishing!* It was spearing and *catching fish!* In the dark! I could see the luminous spear-thrusts and the gulping follow-ups.

This was another heron synchronicity, with another million-to-one-chance against its happening. How many *dozens of alternate fishing spots* did the local herons have, who flew considerable distances from their nests or roosts in order to feed? Waterways were abundant in this area, *in every direction.* Yet here was a heron fishing directly in front of where I was sitting. I didn't even know herons could see in the dark! I was stunned!

As I sat watching, transfixed, *another heron flew up and landed next to the first!* Now there were *two luminous, vertical, dancing snakes, gesticulating before my half-blind vision.* I got the impression that the two herons were greeting one another in a heron ritual. Even though I could still only see the luminous neck and breast plumes, there was a solemn, formal, gestural quality to their motions. They wandered back and forth a few yards away, and eventually disappeared under the city pier. To this day, I don't know how any light at all could enter that covered and enclosed space, the pier jutting out from another breakwater. Yet as they began to disappear from view, I could still see them spearing as they advanced, apparently catching their prey in the black waters. Eventually the two herons emerged again from beneath the dock and gesticulated some more.

By now, I had been watching them for about twenty or thirty minutes, still as a statue. I had seen enough. It was time to leave. I stood up, held my arms aloft, and once again whispered, "Thank you!" to the herons and the mysteries of the night, drove home and went to bed.

I place this entire heron-experience under the heading of the "Cow Skull Burial." When I consider it as a whole, it all strikes me as so incredibly synchronistic, so profoundly meaningful, that to reduce it to a series of fragments, as if they were separate, is a violation of something sacred. How could I cut it into pieces? I cannot. The experience bespeaks an integrity, a coherence of *mind and world* that defies our over-confident, mechanistic rationalizations.

As I mull over this experience for the umpteenth time, my attention is drawn to the crucial turning point, that moment when the mysterious "unseen hand" reached out, crossed my path and *intervened in my life* by turning the steering wheel of my truck one way instead of the other—guiding me, not in the direction of my intention, but in the direction of my fate. Of course, it was my arms and hands, my musculature, my bones and tendons, my own brain and neurons and synapses, that were operating the bulky machine I called the "Red Gorilla." But whatever impulse it was that induced me to obey, the decision was *not a conscious one*. It was an *unconsciously motivated impulse*. But considering how important herons were to me, and how the roles they played in my dreams were mythic roles—to such an extent that I invariably regarded those particular heron dreams as "destiny dreams"—the outcome of that simple unconscious impulse to return to the waterfront instead of proceeding directly home to bed, could not have been more impressive, powerful and portentous.

The *odds against* my encountering a heron—let alone two—*at that precise spot*, which I picked without any forethought, i.e., "at random," and at that *precise time of night,* an uncanny *exactitude of timing* that was an "accidental" result of having carried out and finished my *improvised* ritual—as I say, the odds against its happening were *astronomical*.

I recognize that, to the modern viewpoint, this all still falls within the category of "nothing but coincidence" or "mere chance." But that perspective neither does any justice to, nor does it in any way account for, the *power and meaningfulness to me of the simultaneity of my meeting with the herons at that moment of the night*. It was an experience for a lifetime, never to be forgotten. For me to dismiss or diminish it on the basis of the modern viewpoint would be the height of foolishness, in my view.

There is one more aspect of this middle-of-the-night heron encounter that is worth mentioning.

I said above that I sat in the park, in the dark, through long minutes of puzzlement, and *still did not know what I was seeing*. I could only say that it looked like a "luminous, vertical, dancing snake," and that's the truth. When I finally I realized what I was seeing—the serpentine neck of a Great Blue Heron with its reflective, white neck-plumes—it was the dim and distant light emanating from the *mercury-vapor* street-lamp in front of the police station that brought the heron to the threshold of visibility. That's rational causality—the modernist's religion—at work.

But just as our bodies carry evolutionary history from the cosmic down to the cellular, molecular, atomic and sub-atomic levels, so also *the words we use* carry an evolutionary history. Having evolved from, and among, animals, and despite all our assumed superiority and dominion, we humans can even squawk like animals, if taken by surprise. Exclamatory animal utterances, like "Awwwk!" or "Grrrr!" or "Rrroaow!" can come rising up from our vibrating throats as if we were ravens, walruses or bears.

On a human linguistic level, if we speak of "ballistics" in military hardware, for example, or the "throw-weight" capabilities of missiles, we also invoke the ancient Greek root, *ballein,* to throw, in effect harking back in an unbroken chain, past the Romans, past the Greeks, to the earliest humans or proto-humans, the so-called *hominids,* for all of whom the ballistic activity of "throwing rocks" would probably have been a daily occurrence, whatever the first syllables attached to the stony object and the inevitable action of heaving it might have been.

By that same historical token, if we speak of mercury-vapor, or *vaporized mercury* in the modern, technological sense—like street lamps—we are also making a veiled, unintentional historical reference to the "volatilized Mercury" of the old alchemists. Mercury, of course, was one of the key elements that entered into the metallurgical experiments and symbolic[21] operations of the medieval alchemists—crucial to their *opus*. Although their work did involve actual materials and metals, their esoteric goal was the *transformation of the alchemist himself or herself*. In fact, they considered mercury, i.e., *Mercurius*, to be an embodiment of their *guiding spirit of transformation;* hence their references to the *spiritus mercurius,* a "volatile" spirit capable of flight. They referred to the *serpens mercurii,* the elusive, volatile mercurial serpent, which is how mercury was often depicted in the alchemical manuscripts—a dragon, i.e., a snake with *wings,* which symbolized its vaporized state, its volatility or ability to fly (from Latin *volare,* " to fly"). Or they depicted a snake with a crown, or a "redeeming" snake nailed to a cross, or a snake or dragon biting its tail (the Ouroboros), to symbolize the entire opus, the beginning and the end, the first and the last, the highest and the lowest, etc. Another epithet was *mercurius duplex,* due to the *androgynous* nature of this elusive spirit— Mercurius could manifest in *either masculine or feminine form* (cf. the heron-woman and heron-man of my early heron dreams). These were all symbolic images that spoke to the mystery, to the conjunction of opposites in the energic phenomena the alchemists pursued in their explorations.

Rationally speaking, since so many modern streetlights run an electric arc through vaporized mercury to generate a bright light, my experience that night thus can be rationalistically depreciated as one more *nothing but.* That old reductive reflex again.

But you could also speak more *imaginatively* and say that I was having an *alchemical experience* in the modern world. The volatilized mercury of the *serpens mercurii* shone forth, then was reflected out of primordial darkness in the form of a vertical, luminous, dancing serpent. A vision. Then it underwent a transformation to reveal itself as a Great Blue Heron, a god of the Egyptians, able to see into the darkness, like intuition, like a spirit-being.

In a sense, that mercurial heron was serving me as a mystic guide through the darkness of the unconscious. Now that I think of it, the reflecting neck plumes might also have been serving double duty as a *long-distance beacon* to the other heron, letting it know where to fly, and guiding it to its landing spot on the beach. No wonder the two herons seemed to be bowing and nodding to one another politely, in their serpentine luminosity, their ritual of greeting and obeisance. *How did the second heron know where the first heron was?*

Having written this last paragraph, I am once again reminded how much our comprehension of one another's words depends on which frames of reference we happen to be using, which typologies we employ, how active our imaginations are, what our relations to *soul* might be.

The modern scientific-technological perspective doesn't get me into the intensely felt meanings and emotions *of my own experience*. But depth psychology and alchemy, dreams and their symbolisms, words and their etymologies, most emphatically do.

Please note: By no means am I rejecting science, which for the most part I respect. I only reject the *absolutism* of its universal claim to knowledge. Once again, Jung phrased it well:

> Science is the tool of the Western mind and
> with it more doors can be opened than with
> bare hands. It is part and parcel of our
> knowledge and obscures our insight only when
> it holds that the understanding given by it is the
> only kind there is.

There is one *scientific detail* about this nighttime heron episode that I especially appreciate. After leaving Puget Sound and moving to New Mexico, I had an appointment for a new eyeglass prescription. The optometrist happened to be from Louisiana, upon hearing which I mentioned that he must have seen many herons there. He said he had indeed. Then I mentioned my experience of seeing the heron hunting in the dark the night of the cow-skull burial (I didn't mention that aspect). He told me that the eyes of herons, like those of other night-seeing hunters (e.g., mice, cats, deer, dogs, etc.), are equipped with something called a *tapetum lucidem,* a layer of light-reflecting cells inside the eyeball, part of the retina—like aluminum foil. The *tapetum lucidem,* by multiplying the number of times a stream of photons bounces back and forth inside the eye, effectively magnifies the light-gathering capacity of those eyes, far beyond what the human eye is capable of. He said that to these animals—herons included—a full-moon night, which is only dimly lit to us, would be like daylight to them.

So, the *volatilized mercury* reflecting off the neck and breast plumes of the heron really could have served as a beacon to the second heron, and they both would have been able to see the little wiggling delicacies in the waters at their feet. For all I know, there might have been some *phosphorescent effect* as well, as the fish moved about in the water, lighting them up like flares so the herons with their night-vision *tapetum lucidem* could strike and swallow them whole. A delicious midnight snack

Because it is my nature to do so, I use that tiny bit of scientific knowledge to amplify the mythological, intuitive knowledge that guided me in the dark to the herons, who were my spirit-guides. Modern science would not have done that. In fact, I suspect that modern science would have counseled me to forget the ritual altogether. Don't bother, Paco. Stay asleep.

As I said above, the heron dreams I recorded were powerful but not many in number, maybe a dozen or fewer, spread over a period of years. Naturally, throughout those years I kept up my daily reconnaissance missions of "spotting" herons in their various haunts around the beaches and local lagoons—standing on one leg on top of pilings, digesting; or asleep with their beaks under a wing; flying overhead; and so forth. I became an expert at spotting herons in all kinds of locations, and the birds were usually solitary. On one occasion, however, I had taken a cross-sound ferry and was driving toward the mainland on a road that overlooked a vast mudflat, when I saw *herons everywhere*. A bonanza of herons that extended far into the distance, like nothing I had ever seen!

I stopped my car and tried several times to count them. Each time the count reached 100 herons, I lost count and gave up counting. There were *too many* of them to count! What were they doing in such numbers? I knew they were feeding, of course, on the low-tide mudflats, but what else were they doing? Was this an annual heron picnic, like the children's song of the Teddy-Bear Picnic? Were they holding a Grand Heron-Courtship Festival? I amused myself with different notions. Maybe they were holding a convention, to elect officers for the coming year. Or maybe they...

The Heron Guardians

ABOUT TWENTY YEARS AFTER RECORDING YET ANOTHER MAJOR heron dream, I "re-entered" that particular dream, only this time I was awake, using a technique that Jung invented and called, "active imagination," which he also referred to as "Dreaming the dream onward." This particular active imagination almost had the quality of a *cosmic vision*, and, combined with other dreams and experiences I've had, it added to my unusual perspective on life and death. In the dream:

> *I am walking alone through an empty cityscape.*
> *I carry a bow and arrow with me—an archaic*
> *technology going back at least 60,000 years.*[22]
> *Periodically I shoot the arrow, run after it and*
> *pick it up wherever it lands. Then I shoot it*
> *again and run after it again. After several*
> *repetitions of this, the arrow lands near the*
> *body of a dead heron. This stuns me. I run over*
> *to the heron, then immediately I see another*
> *one, also dead. Then another. They are spaced*
> *in such a way that I realize I am being led along*
> *a trail of dead herons. The trail leads me to an*
> *opening in some dense shrubbery, like a narrow*

tunnel. I enter the tunnel and find two or three more dead herons, also spaced out along the trail, as if leading me onward. I continue until I am crawling, the tunnel has gotten so low. Then suddenly it opens up into a larger space, like a gallery will sometimes open up in a large cavern. I stand up.

Before me I see a large, formal door, on both sides of which stand two fierce and resplendent herons. The herons are quite alive, exuding vitality and shimmering with iridescent, peacock colors. I might even say they are "super-alive." But, amazingly, they are also heron statues, i.e., fixed sculptures. They are alive, yet not alive. I might say they are "living artifacts." In their presentation they remind me of Chinese tomb guardians, which are also placed on either side of a tomb opening, and are crafted with life-like, though stylized, ferocity, presented as if they were alive. Their function is to frighten off evil spirits, to protect the soul of the deceased. Is that the purpose of these two marvelous herons? To ward off danger? To welcome visitors? Or?

As I look at the two "heron guardians," I realize something about the doorway. It is an intuitive realization, I'm sure, something one can only "know" through intuition. On the other side of this door lies The Realm of Absolute Reality! Or I could also call it The Realm of Pure Potential. There are probably lots of other names for it, but those are the names that come to me in the dream.

There is something else. I feel that, if I were to open the door and cross over the threshold, I would in some sense be "dead," at least in the sense that I know myself to be "alive" on this side of the door. If I were to cross the threshold, "I" would cease to exist. At the minimum, this is

103

an image of a complete ego-death. At least,
that's how it seems to me in the dream. Frankly,
I do not want to "die" by opening the door and
crossing the threshold. But then, at that point
the brambles forming the tunnel seem to come
alive, like they sometimes do in fairy tales, and
the brambly "room" begins to shrink around
me. I do not cross the threshold. [End of
dream.]

As soon as I woke up, I wrote down the dream.

Pondering the fascinating images, I realized that everything made a strange kind of sense. I shoot an *arrow* and follow it. Not because I am "hunting" as such, but simply to follow the arrow where it leads, which is a different kind of hunt—*a quest for something unknown*. This struck me as a *pun*. I was following my arrows—that is, following my *eros*, which is what I had been doing for years. That's what I was doing when I ran after the wild dream-horses that led me to the dead heron whose beak was a "special writing instrument." The trail I was following this time was leading me deeper into the "underworld," away from the day-world of conventional consciousness and life, toward the realm of the dead, the spirit-realm. This is an archaic conception, I know, but that doesn't mean that there was never anything to it, in archaic times, or that it doesn't still have some value, some *punch* for our modern lives today, just because we dismiss it out of hand as "superstitious." To me, that's an intellectual conceit that shows our limitations.

And here's another curiosity about the course the dream took: the farther along the trail of dead herons I went, and the more removed I became from the day-world, the more alive and vivid the dream became. Until I reached the door with the two "heron guardians" who were, in some uncanny way, *more than alive,* or, as I put it, "super-alive"—and yet non-living "statues" at the same time. My progress through the dream— which led me into and through the tunnel to "The Door"— brought me to the threshold of what I knew would be *Absolute Reality*, or something like it. While dreaming, I didn't find out what would *really* happen if I crossed the threshold, but for years I thought about that dream, mulling it over and over.

Periodically, I would think about crossing the threshold and wonder what would happen.

One day I was lying down, reading, thinking about dreams and active imagination. Suddenly, the "heron guardians" dream popped into my head—twenty years after it had occurred—and I decided to go back into it, in an *active imagination*. This time, however, I decided I was going to *cross the threshold*!

I put the book down, closed my eyes, and in my imagination I "actively" re-entered the brambled dream-cave at the clearing, approached the formidable door, opened it and stepped across the threshold into the so-called "absolute realm of non-contingency," or, as I also thought about it: "pure potential."

Instantly, I found myself zooming at great speed through the blackness of what seemed like outer space. Some black birds flapped toward me, as if to frighten me off, it seemed. They appeared almost comical, and I brushed them aside. I continued zooming, but then thought to myself, "Why am I zooming through outer space like this? I want to go back to the door and look across the threshold *from this side, the "other side."* No sooner did I think or imagine this than it happened. I approached the opening to the doorway, looking back toward the bramble-cave, and was shocked to see that "I" was still standing there, still on the other side! *I saw myself, standing on the other side of the threshold*—a sincere, imperfect person, the questing pilgrim, always seeking. I felt a wave of love for this person *who was myself*—in his "worldly aspect," I suppose. I stepped over the threshold again, back to *his* side—the contingent side—and embraced him. I felt a deep love for him, and always had. Then I put my hands on his shoulders and turned him around, gently pushing him back through the tunnel, back toward the world of the living. I walked close to him, matching my footsteps with his. We walked in tandem, foot for foot, step for step. Then I floated upward, hovering over him, and accompanied him out of the tunnel. *I knew that I had always been with him, and I would always be with him.*

When I came out of the vision I was weeping, deeply moved. I don't know if anything like this would have happened had I crossed the threshold twenty years earlier, while still in the original dream. Perhaps not. But I was obviously not ready back then. This time I was ready, but was surprised to have had what is commonly reported in "the literature" as an OBE—an out-of-body experience. These and similar experiences are well enough documented to leave little doubt about the *elasticity* of the psyche, that is, its *relativity* in relationship to time and space. The deeper into the unconscious psyche we go, the more relativized things become. That is one reason why, if we try to apply literal, rational and materialistic expectations to dreams, where psychic relativity applies, we cannot do justice to dreams.

As Jung said in his autobiography:

> I have become convinced that at least part of our psychic existence is characterized by the relativity of space and time. This relativity seems to increase, in proportion to the distance from consciousness, to an absolute condition of timelessness and spacelessness. (MDR, p. 305.)

The outcome of my spontaneous, active-imagination experiment—twenty years after the dream itself—confirmed what I had intuited in the original dream about "the other side of the threshold." I had indeed entered some *imaginal, as-if unqualified, non-contingent state or realm*, and the notion of "pure potential," which had come to me in the original dream, seemed to suit it quite well. What should I call *what I experienced in the active imagination"* An *epiphany*? An *angelophany*? Either term will do. But by whatever name, the experience has altered my views about the nature of reality, even touching on the relations between life and death—a topic for another effort. But another intriguing question remains to this day: *Who was I, when I stood on the "other" side of the threshold, looking back at "myself"?*

I have ideas about that, but I prefer—for now—to leave question and its mystery hovering in the air.

PART THREE

Return **to Caborca**

One Beak in Hand, Two Realities Conjoined

THE DREAM OF HOLDING THE HERON'S BEAK AS A "SPECIAL writing instrument," set me on the course of *taking writing seriously*, but without telling me *what to write*. So, I began writing essays on things that were on my mind at the time, having to do with aspects of dreams and synchronicities that had caught my attention, thanks to the illuminating insights yielded by Jung's profound depth psychology. This all took place when I was still living in Puget Sound, so rich for me in my voluntary near-poverty—what with the dreams, herons and sunrises-over-water it afforded me.

As for the writing, I was especially interested in how *certain dream images*—especially animals in dreams—might be regarded as "angels." As I pondered this odd question, I was wondering: Did the "angels" of ancient traditions ever pertain to actual phenomena, actual experiences? Why were traditional depictions and accounts of angels or other spirit-beings so *ubiquitous,* so trans-cultural, in ancient times? Was it just because people were so *superstitious* back then, whereas we are so *superior* today? (I doubted that.) Do angels manifest the existence of *psychic agencies and energies inherent in the cosmos,* independent of traditional belief systems, of the ego's will or of scientific dominance? (That seemed possible.) Does the universality of angels point to some *inherent function within the human psyche*? (That also seemed possible—and more likely to me than the traditional, *literal* notions of angels, tied as they are to theological doctrines increasingly open to dispute, especially vulnerable to scientific criticisms.)

The fact that angels and other spirit-beings were common to practically all archaic cultures and religions, suggests to me that they must have been *about something, like some real agency capable of entering the field of human experience, both temporal and spatial, hence capable of presenting itself to consciousness, and actively intervening therein.*

At any rate, angel-like beings far pre-dated any developed theologies, or even writing. I concluded that there must have been *many compelling experiences* from the very earliest prehistorical, even paleolithic, times, as for instance, when the tribal healers—women and/or men—brought cultural and medicinal knowledge to their tribes through the intermediary actions of spirit guides, through dreams, induced trances and spontaneous or hallucinogenic visions. Those guides often took the form of *animal spirits.* Hence, shamanic powers commonly involved the ability to communicate with the animals.[23, 24]

While following up on the *heron's-beak writing dream,* I had also been writing down memories from my early childhood—as many as I could possibly recall. Then one afternoon, when I sat down to write, it struck me that *I had never written anything about the experience of losing my eye in Mexico.* So, I decided to do that. I wrote one paragraph. The process was interesting, intriguing, fascinating. So, I wrote a second paragraph.

Then the dam broke. I wrote virtually non-stop—morning, noon and night—for six straight weeks. By the time I stopped writing and the dust settled, I had accumulated 96 pages of text. I realized that I had the core of a book in my hands.

More importantly, I also realized with a shudder that *I had to go back to Mexico*—back to Caborca, the place I never wanted to see again—not that I ever really *saw* it the first time.

But I could not possibly complete what had erupted so spontaneously into my life as "the Caborca project"—*six weeks of writing and 96 pages*—without also *going back to the place where the accident had occurred.* It was the same feeling of solemn obligation that I felt when I realized I had to carry out the ritual on the Tooth Beach at low tide, to bury the cow skull, with the simple, solemn, eulogistic message I had written across the white forehead.

When I completed those six weeks of writing, however, November had arrived in Puget Sound, a dark and dreary season. The combination of this time of near-perpetual darkness, plus the deep grief I was feeling while bringing up intense memories of Caborca (at least the memories I had retained), and a fearsome dread of returning to what felt like it would result in an *inevitable death*—maybe permanent this time—all this opened the valves to the "waterworks," so to speak, and I sobbed for two days, so much unconscious emotion had been released by the writing. I was sobbing in part because *I knew that I could not avoid making the return trip*. I was in the grip of a *daimon* that was making its demand upon me, just as the six-foot-tall heron-man had done in the dream, when it demanded, in Italian, to be fed. So, I felt I had no choice. Like it or not, I *had* to go. Therefore, I *would* go.

Then I realized that, although I had to return to Caborca, I didn't have to return just then, in dark, deadly November. I could go after the New Year, instead. In fact, I could go in the Spring. I could even make the trip during Easter, the symbolic season of death and resurrection, of the Spring Equinox and its return of spring's life after winter's death, light after dark, life after death. My spirits rose with this realization, and I began making plans for the trip.

A Promise

ALL OF THE ABOVE CONSIDERATIONS—the accident, the visions, the herons, the dreams, the insights, the synchronistic events, the thoughts about angels, and even the process of writing about them all—had brought me to this point: I would now, after so many years, actually return to the fearsome precincts of Caborca.

In one of Jung's volumes, in his essay on "The Psychology of the Divine Child," he wrote a passage that has stuck with me ever since I first read it. I felt the truth of it in my bones then, and I still do. The *motif of the divine child* represents, he said:

> ...the strongest, the most ineluctable urge in every being, namely the urge to realize itself. It is, as it were, an incarnation of the *inability to do otherwise*, equipped with all the powers of nature and instinct, whereas the conscious mind is always getting caught up in its supposed ability to do otherwise. [Emphasis added.]

Something along these lines had come into play and was forcing this paradoxical decision on me—a decision I resisted and welcomed at the same time. Personally, I did not want to return. I wanted "to do otherwise." Yet the deeper, better part of me knew it was absolutely necessary, and it was therefore "the right thing to do." I suppose that's what fate, or destiny, sometimes feels like.

So, despite my longstanding determination never to return to Mexico, I no longer had any choice in the matter. For, in the course of more than 27 years of searching, of diving into the shadows, of digging in the quarries of dreams and visions, of conflict and desire, of wounding, illumination and distress, I had extracted a few tiny nuggets of precious gold, which I had hammered and polished until each one, however thin, shone like a mirror, reflecting back to me the sun of my own obscure truth.

It was precisely the light of this inner truth that now told me I must return to the place of my wounding, of my near-death experience, the place of my initiation into the dark mysteries of the psyche. There to place one more cross along Highway 2, as a simple way of marking the point of my awakening. To memorialize the place of sacrifice. To consecrate a piece of ground, a spot in the desert 10 miles west of Caborca. I would inscribe the cross with a few simple words in Spanish, the adopted language of my soul, and I would sign it, "Paco Mitchell."

112

Many will wonder why I would even bother. Why go to all that trouble and expense after all these years? The cow is dead. The boy who lost his eye is metaphorically "dead" as well. It was just an accident. Who even remembers? Who cares? To these I must say: I care.

As I tended these memories like a sacred fire in my soul, what emerged from the flames of death, fear and loss was . . . a feeling of intense love! After all this pain, this prolonged ordeal, with its wounding and healing, forgetting and remembering, losing and finding, I was left with a feeling of love for Caborca, for the cow that died, for the *zopilotes* hunched over the cow's carcass. Love for the Mexican doctor who signed my medical release, and for José the pilot, who air-lifted me out of Caborca that same day. Love for my mother who responded without hesitation to Phil's call. Love for Phil himself, who saved my life with his gutsy determination and hell-for-broke pidgin-Spanish. Love for the *Cuerpo de Ambulantes de la Cruz Roja de Caborca* (Carlos Pino, Luis Jaime, Juan Antonio Rivera, Miguel Angel Morales, Germán Contreras Pino, Jornulfo Gómez, Felipardo Martínez Callezda, Billy Ortega, Ricardo Partillo, Leonardo Elias Jaime, and Paulino Sánchez. I had their signatures on the old photograph in front of me.) Love for whoever arranged the *mordida* to expedite Phil's timely release and departure from Caborca. Love for the dirt and heat, the cactus and sizzling macadam. Love for the eye lost and the vision gained. Love for the psyche that arranges the fateful events of our lives and contrives to bring us to greater awareness in spite of ourselves. Love for the dreams that always know what I don't, even though they don't always say it in ways I can understand.

Love for the luminous snake that drew me down into the depths, tricked me repeatedly along the way, and then turned into a bird-man to guide me back up and out again.

And so, early the next year, in 1991, the 28th year after my initiation, I would return to Caborca. That was my promise.

PART **FOUR**

Ritual Beauty

> The beauty of the ritual action is one of its essential properties, for man has not served God rightly unless he has also served him in beauty.[25]
>
> —C. G. Jung

The Amazing Well of Grief

THE EMOTIONS THAT CAME TO ME THAT AFTERNOON WERE POWERFUL, and I sat with them, poring over the photograph of the Cruz Roja ambulance drivers, going deeper into the amazing well of grief than I ever had before, a well whose existence I knew nothing about as a youth.

Then something new began to happen, like an offshoot growing out of the taproot of love I was feeling. It was as if the love I had already begun to experience opened like a "mystical rose," as the saying goes. I actually felt myself being drawn forward, as the trip began to form in my imagination. I saw myself meeting some of the men in the photograph and shaking their hands, going to the Caborca hospital, searching out José the pilot, driving out into the desert to place the cross—and my emotions began to differentiate: Out of the watery depths of fear, grief and dread, there now rose not only love, but also a buoyancy, almost a passion, for the place and the event that had given such meaning to my life.

La Cruz Blanca

I PUZZLED OVER WHAT TO DO ABOUT THE CROSS.[26] Should I make it here or in Caborca? Should it be milled lumber or rough sticks? Painted or bare? How big? Should I carry it assembled or disassembled? What kind of a joint should it have? All the normal concerns of a carpenter, artist or artisan.

Since I was simply thinking in terms of personal gratitude to something I didn't understand but knew was greater than myself—rather than any convoluted religious doctrine like penitence or the *imitatio Christi*—I didn't want to drag a huge cross through the airports and bus terminals of North America with bleeding knees, lashing my back with a knotted leather flail. I was not re-enacting the crucifixion, not offering myself as a candidate for nailing, not travelling the Via Dolorosa to Golgotha, the Hill of Skulls.

Others would have to serve that penitential and mimetic function, re-enacting the mythic drama by undergoing the same torments suffered by the God-Man. Others would have to flail themselves and walk on their knees to atone for their sins and the sins of others.

No, I was making a simple gesture of thanks, acknowledging an immense debt to forces I did not understand, and which had come to be symbolized by a dead cow, a town called Caborca, and some faces in a photograph.

So I made a simple, white wooden cross on my table saw, *una cruz blanca*, with a simple cross-lap joint and pre-drilled, countersunk pilot holes, something light and easy to carry that wouldn't violate the touchy mental categories of airline and border officials in the charged security atmosphere of international boundaries.

Something I could assemble on the spot in Caborca. I would pack a little wood-glue in my suitcase, along with some countersunk-head screws and a Philips-head screwdriver—called a *cruz* in Spanish. A cross.

Shortly before my departure I sat down at the computer and a simple poem came to mind, in Spanish.

116

It was like a prayer. I wrote it down as it came to me:

UNA CRUZ PARA CABORCA	A CROSS FOR CABORCA
En este sitio,	On this site,
O muy cerca de aquí,	Or very close to here,
El 10 de septiembre	On the tenth of September,
De 1963,	1963,
Hubo un accidente	There was an accident
En que un automóvil	In which an automobile
Se chocó con	Collided with
Una vaca.	A cow.
Se murió la vaca.	The cow died.
Se destrozó el auto.	The car was destroyed.
Y un jóven perdió	And a young man lost
Un ojo.	An eye.
Hoy,	Today,
Veintiocho años después,	Twenty-eight years later,
He vuelto yo,	I have returned,
Jóven que ya no soy	That same man but no longer a
Jóven,	Youth,
Poseedor de un solo ojo.	Possessing only one eye.
He vuelto aquí	I have returned here
A Sonora	To Sonora
Para erigir	In order to erect
Esta cruz humilde,	This humble cross
De madera blanca,	Of white wood,
Rodeada de un pirámide de piedras,	Surrounded by a pyramid of stones
Para darle gracias	In order to give thanks
Al Ser Supremo	To the Supreme Being
Por haberme permitido	For having granted me

Y la supervivencia	Both survival
Y la vista interior.	And inner vision.
La cruz también se dedica	The cross is also dedicated
A la vaca que murió,	To the cow that died,
Una vaca negra,	A black cow,
Animal muda y piedosa,	A mute and pious animal,
Que sufrió	Who suffered
Sin conocimiento,	Without understanding,
Sin saber nada	Without knowing anything
Del bueno que hacía,	Of the good it was doing,
Nada de la vista	Nothing of the vision
Que me daba	It was bestowing upon me
Al mismo momento	At the very moment
En que la vista	In which it was taking my sight
Me sacaba.	Away from me.
Y usted:	And you:
¿Pasajero, caminante,	Passerby, pedestrian,
Peregrino?	Pilgrim?
¿Qué dice usted?	What do you say?
¿Qué va usted a dejar aquí?	What will you leave here?
¿Desprecio, risas,	Scorn? Laughter?
El olvido?	Forgetfulness?
¿O tal vez quiere usted	Or perhaps would you like
Ayudarme un poco	To help me a little
Con la memoria,	With this memorial,
Contribuír	And contribute
Una piedra más	One more stone
Al pirámide	To the pyramid
Que se va formando aquí,	That is taking shape here,
Para que se estableciera	In order to establish
En el desierto	In the desert

| *Un pedacito* | A little piece |
| *De tierra sagrada?* | Of sacred ground? |

I arranged the Spanish version of the poem in a narrow column, reduced it to the smallest typeface I had, cut it into a strip, and laminated it to the upright member of the cross with a clear resin compound. Once the resin had cured, I wrapped the cross in black plastic, unassembled, and taped the package with white cloth tape. I would probably have to check it as baggage at the airport. It reminded me of a long thin mummy.

As the departure date drew nearer, I noticed my energy and attention being drawn more strongly forward, like a boat being pulled toward some massive, distant maelstrom. This was more than the normal preoccupation with airline tickets, traveler's cheques and how many changes of socks I would need. It was a pull downward, a sense of increasing gravity, as if a portion of my psyche was being detached from my little boat and drawn ahead of it, already disappearing into the crashing maelstrom.

I began to spend more time consulting the Mexican travel books I had found, reading and re-reading the brief entry on Caborca like a Catholic reciting the "Hail Mary." I wrote a letter in Spanish to the Red Cross in Caborca, telling them of my intention to go there, and the date I would arrive. I had no idea whether the letter would ever get delivered, or whether anyone would pay attention to it. I had no address for the Red Cross—remember, no Google, no Internet then—so I simply sent it to: *Cruz Roja de Caborca. Caborca, Sonora, México.*

I hoped someone would get it.

Two days before I left, a *stranger* came to my door. He identified himself as a childhood neighbor of my wife. He had lived down the street from her when her family moved from New Mexico to Oregon, *thirty-five years earlier*. He had been in the fourth grade; she was in the eighth grade. She vaguely remembered him or pretended she did. In the course of our conversation the stranger mentioned that his daughter was in Mexico helping to build a church, a missionary project of some sort. His conversation was all church-this and church-that. But after a few minutes I began to feel a strange sensation, hair rising on my neck. Finally, I asked where in Mexico his daughter was. His wife answered the question for him. She said: "Caborca."

The effect on me was like a huge blade plunging down from overhead, splintering the table where we sat. I listened to their story with a mixture of excitement and dread, pumping them for information on Caborca. They knew next to nothing about it. No matter, the message had been delivered. *In the twenty-eight years since the accident, no one had ever once mentioned the name "Caborca" to me.* Nor had I ever come across the name in print. Several times I had even looked at different maps of Mexico and could not find it! Very few people had even heard of it. The "coincidence" of this stranger coming into my house from out of nowhere on the eve of my return trip, bearing news of Caborca, confirmed my suspicion that "Caborca" was indeed a symbol for some large *world-ordering process* whose power and magnitude were far beyond my ken, but *to which my life was somehow subject.* Whatever force it was that could arrange such a meaningful coincidence on the eve of my departure, must have had powerful resources indeed to bring to bear upon individual lives and the tapestries of fate in which those lives are interwoven. With this stranger's arrival in my home two days before my departure, I felt that "Caborca" no longer belonged only to me personally, but now in some strange way belonged to the world.

Here Goes Nothing

ON THURSDAY, MAY **28, 1991,** I FINALLY SET OUT FOR CABORCA. It would take two days to get there. My objective the first day was to reach Tucson, Arizona, stay in a motel, and travel to Caborca the next day. I rose early and made my way to the airport. I was not sure how my cross would be received by the airline officials. At the check-in counter I held up the long, narrow parcel and asked the airline agent if I could carry it on board. He asked me what it was. "A wooden cross," I said. He answered, "No." I asked if I could check it as baggage, to which he replied, "Sure." To my black plastic and white tape he then added his own decorations in the form of routing stickers, ID tags and a spiral winding of white and red tape. What began as a long, thin mummy, now looked like a four-foot candy cane. When he finished, he carefully placed it in a tray on the conveyor belt, next to my suitcase, and said, with aplomb: "One bag. One cross." Apparently his sense of drama and humor had not been dulled by years of dealing with harassed, impatient travelers.

My itinerary took me unexpectedly through Los Angeles International Airport and from there to Tucson. On the flight to Tucson I sat next to a Mexican fellow. I spoke Spanish with him, wanting to practice before crossing the border. I told him about my mission and asked if he knew anything about Caborca. He told me what little he knew, and we talked about his job, his wife's fear of Los Angeles earthquakes, the ins and outs of travel in Mexico. We talked about Mexican officialdom and the problem of bribes. He gave me a warning: "Don't trust anybody." As we parted, he wished me luck on my journey. We shook hands and I stepped into the desert air of an Arizona night.

I called for a ride to a nearby motel. The driver's name was Eduardo. He also was from Mexico and had been to Caborca. I was getting closer. We spoke in Spanish.

He described how I would get to the Nogales, Mexico bus terminal from the border checkpoint. He thought there might be several buses a day running to Caborca. I asked him the Spanish term for

"crop-duster." He said: *"Avión fumigador."* I would need that later on. More handshakes and well-wishing. I liked Eduardo. He liked the fact that I spoke Spanish.

121

The Big Bang

If we compare the news of an event to a bomb, we can say that the stranger walking into my house telling me about his daughter in Caborca was a conventional explosive, like a hand-grenade lobbed in the direction of a foxhole. Soon after settling into my motel room in Tucson, however, I met with the full force of a multi-megaton nuclear device, detonating over ground-zero. I called my wife to let her know I had made it safely to Tucson, only to find out she had been trying to reach me: *My mother had just been killed in an automobile accident.*

It had happened a few hours earlier, while I was flying into Los Angeles, City of the Angels. My wife couldn't tell me any of the details, which only emerged gradually, as the piecemeal story came together over the next few days. Teenagers racing inland from the beach at around four in the afternoon. 100 + miles per hour on a four-lane boulevard. Passing other cars on the shoulder. Spinning out of control. A violent, head-on impact with my mother's car at a combined speed of about 140 miles per hour or more. Three wheels torn off my mother's car, which landed on its side. Six ambulances, two helicopters and three fire trucks on the scene.

Traffic blocked for hours. My sister, who had been driving the car, was unconscious. My mother's heart was torn open by the impact. She died instantly. They airlifted her to a hospital, to no avail. DOA.

Since my sister was driving, they hit her side of the car. Miraculously, she survived, with multiple fractures of her left arm, muscle and nerve damage from the gashes, impaired motion in her left hand and arm—possibly permanent—two broken ribs, a cracked jaw, a concussion, assorted lacerations, abrasions and deep bruises. It was several hours before she could remember what had happened. There wasn't even time to yell. She and my mother were on their way to get flowers for her daughter's wedding.

The nineteen-year-old driver of the other vehicle was uninjured. His girlfriend, whose car it was, almost lost an arm. One passenger had a crushed pelvis. Another had a broken back. The driver is up for Vehicular Homicide, his five-mile joyride ending in a lifetime of sorrow.

I am hesitant to say even this much about my mother's death, partly out of respect for her soul, partly from reticence before the inscrutable mystery of Death, and partly because the emotions, even today, are never far from the surface, joined as they are with the entire Caborca phenomenon. Yet I had to include at least these few details of the event, which immediately formed an important—even crucial—part of my experience in returning to Caborca and the ritual I performed there. I do not want to speculate publicly on the bizarre coincidence of her death with the day of my departure, but I cannot omit this painful event from the fateful Caborca mosaic. Suffice it to say that fate is indeed a life-and-death matter, and my mother's death was a *synchronistic piece of the pattern*.

After hearing the news, I made several phone calls to relatives. No one had had a chance to arrange the funeral. My two brothers lived in the mountains above San Bernardino, above Los Angeles, but there had been a freak, unseasonal snowstorm that blocked the highway off the mountain and the power lines were down. No one knew when the highway would be open again, or when the requisite autopsy (Vehicular Homicide) would take place. We were all up in the air.

So, since no one knew anything yet, and after much deliberation, I decided to make the trip to Caborca and return sooner than planned, in order to attend the funeral—whenever it could be arranged. It was sure to be a quick and arduous journey, intense in all respects. Once all the phone calls were finished, I was in a state of shock. I lay down on the motel room bed and tried to rest. I was numb and agitated with travel fatigue and emotion. Fortunately, I had brought a tape recording of Faure's *Requiem*—the piece of music that I played constantly during those first six weeks of writing about Caborca. Once again, I played it over and over to accompany me in my grief into the early morning hours. With some difficulty, I finally fell asleep, but just barely.

An hour or so later I was disturbed by the booming growl of a man's voice in the hallway right outside my room. A smoking cowboy from the sound of his loud, gravelly voice and his accent. Did he know what time it was? Did he realize that people were trying to sleep? Apparently not. It was four-thirty AM—but once awake I couldn't go back to sleep. So, I finally rose, showered and went downstairs for breakfast, trying to gather my wits for the upcoming trip. I called for a taxi, and headed for the Tucson bus station, about 20 minutes away. Since there was no air or rail service to either Caborca or Nogales, and since in those days I couldn't rent a car in Arizona and take it across the border, I would have to travel from the motel to the Tucson Greyhound bus station by taxi, then from Tucson to Nogales by bus, walk across the border, then take a Mexican bus to Caborca. I had been given conflicting information about how often the Mexican buses left Nogales. One source told me there were three buses a day. Eduardo the shuttle driver thought it was every half-hour. Every time I had tried to phone the Mexican bus company, *Tres Estrellas,* I couldn't get through. I would just have to find out when I got there.

I sat for an hour in the Tucson bus terminal, doing my best to keep a positive attitude in the face of sleep-deprivation, raw emotions, and nerves. I probably drank too much coffee at breakfast. The Greyhound bus finally arrived and loaded, and we left for Nogales and the border. On the way I dictated notes into my pocket tape recorder and wondered what I would be facing in Mexico. The bus droned past rocks, saguaros and pecan orchards, while my body buzzed with grief, fatigue and caffeine. I decided to write a poem for my mother, to read aloud when I planted the cross in Caborca. I wrote it in verse, in Spanish:

LA FORTUNA	FATE
El mismo día en que yo fui	On the very day I went
A Caborca, donde el ojo yo perdí,	To Caborca, where I lost my eye,

124

Un otro choque ocurrió,	Another collision occurred,
Peor que el que el ojo me quitó.	Worse than the one that took away my eye.
Fuí un accidente inadvertido,	It was an accident without warning,
Como es todo lo imprevisto.	As is everything unforeseen
No sé cómo ni por qué ocurrió:	I don't know how or why it happened:
Solamente me dijeron que	They only told me that
Mi madre murió.	My mother had died.
¿Cómo puede ser tal la fortuna,	How can Fate be such, that,
Que, sin ver intención alguna,	Without seeing any reason for it,
Al momento en que la muerte yo seguí	At the moment I was following death,
La muerte me estaba siguiendo a mí?	Death itself was following me?
Supongo que ya no sufre, y que yace	I suppose she no longer suffers, that she's lying
Al lado de mi padre, y que nace	Beside my father, and that now they give birth
Ese amor eterno y divino que,	To that eternal and divine love
Mientras vivían, les servía como destino.	That, while they were alive, served as their destiny.

The last verse came to me as an insight about my parents: that their love was their destiny, that her death fulfilled that love, since now and at last they could be together in eternity, my father having died suddenly of a heart attack in early 1962, a year and a half before the accident in Caborca. With this realization I tapped into a new vein of emotion—half-sorrow, half-joy—at the image of my parents finally re-united. I finished the poem as the bus rolled into the Nogales city limits. I sat there with my notebook and pocket tape recorder, tears streaming down my cheeks, blowing my nose, a blue-eyed pilgrim among all the brown-eyed Mexicans heading home for Easter. I could feel the border getting closer: *casa de cambios, carnicería, faldas y blusas, zapatería, licores, taquería.* We had already passed the linguistic boundary before reaching the border. I recited the Spanish signs aloud, like an incantation. But also, I needed the practice, since there weren't many *hispanoparlantes*—Spanish speakers—in the Puget Sound area where I lived.

PART FIVE
The Descent

Crossing the Border

SOON THE BUS STOPPED, AND ALL THE PASSENGERS SPILLED out into a narrow space between two buildings. I got my luggage and cross and let myself be carried with the current of bodies. We were like a flash flood, a human cataract surging down a concrete arroyo, rushing past stationary pockets of people like water past rocks. Before I had a chance to orient myself, I was over the border and small boys had singled me out as a *gringo* and therefore a source of easy cash. They approached me, offering to carry my bags. Taxi drivers offered rides, or anything else I might need. I knew the bus station was close by, so I shrugged off their offers and plowed through the Good Friday crowds.

Another driver approached, more insistent than the others. He wanted to know where I was going. I answered in Spanish, refusing his offer. I told him I was taking the bus to Caborca. He told me *there weren't any buses to Caborca*. I didn't know whether to believe him or not. He said I could find out for myself; he would wait for me outside the bus station. I squeezed into the small office of the *Tres Estrellas* bus terminal, put down my bags and turned around. The room was crowded and dingy. Every eye in the place was on me and, as on the bus from Tucson, every one of those eyes was brown. Am I the only gringo in Nogales today? I felt tremendously conspicuous, awkward and unknowing, but could hardly afford to be intimidated. I approached a low window, bent down awkwardly and inquired in Spanish about the next bus departure for Caborca.

There was only one. It left at 9:00 in the evening. They didn't know what time it would arrive. Sometime after midnight, probably. I looked at my watch. It was one o'clock in the afternoon. I was faced with eight hours of waiting in this room, or with dragging my suitcase and cross around the streets of Nogales all day, only to take a bus trip of several hours' length, arriving at Caborca sometime in the middle of the night. This was a grim prospect. I sized up the situation, and realized I was snookered. The taxi driver had me over

a barrel and he knew it. I walked back outside and approached the man. He offered to drive me to Caborca for $150. I told him he was surely joking, turning back toward the bus terminal. He then offered to take me to Santa Ana for $50. As I stopped to consider this new offer, he drove the sword in up to the hilt in a clean *estocada*, over the horns, saying in Spanish: *"¡Perdemos tiempo!"* We're wasting time!

It was true. I had precious little time to get to Caborca and accomplish my mission, and still get back in time for the funeral. I couldn't afford to hang around Nogales all day. I agreed to his price. *¡Bueno! ¡Cincuenta dólares! ¡Vámonos!* Let's go!

He led me to his taxi, a dirty black Detroit sedan of indeterminate age and make, probably a Chevy. It sported a white plastic bubble on top that hinted at its status as a taxi. There was no sign on the bubble or the door, no meter, no company logo, no number. For all I knew, this guy could have been an axe murderer. I thought about the advice my Mexican friend had given me on the flight to Tucson: "Don't trust anybody," he had said, referring to the *banditos* and con artists I might run into at the border. I had decided to trust fate, however, and not worry (excessively) about getting driven out of town and being robbed, mugged or murdered, my body dumped in an arroyo.

As I was about to get in, the driver started talking to me and gesturing to a group of people across the street. Is this it? Does the scam begin here? It took several repetitions before I understood what he was saying. A friend of his wanted a ride to Magdalena and did I mind if he came along? Well, I'm either safe here or I'm not safe, and frankly, I can't tell which it is. I'm tired, completely disoriented and a bit stressed. I don't feel safe at all, don't really understand what's going on, but I'm hardly in control of my destiny at this point anyway. Whatever is going to happen to me is going to happen, whether I like it or not, right? So, I say, *"¿Por qué no?"* Why not? Of course, your friend can ride along. After all, a mugging

is a lot more efficient when it's two against one! *¡Vámonos!*
Let's go!

   As we threaded our way through the streets of Nogales, I
decided to take an active approach with my two comrades
and try to build

 some rapport. I engaged them in a conversation in Spanish.
The driver's name was Antonio. His friend's name was
Armando. (He showed me his baseball hat with "Armando"
embroidered on it. I guess that proved it.) Antonio's dad was
about 75 yrs. old, and drove this same taxi on the morning
shift, rising each day at five AM. I told them about the purpose
of my journey, and about my mother's death the day before.
They were both affected by the news, and very sympathetic:
"Lo siento mucho, Paco," Antonio said, expressing his regret.
He told me his own mother had died a year and a half ago,
and that there was "no other pain like it in the world."
Armando agreed, saying: "It makes your heart hurt." I recited
for them the poem I had just written on the bus. We mused
on the mysteries of life and death and talked about Antonio's
two kids. The taxi sped through the desert, lurching and
swaying, while Antonio's good luck charms dangled from the
rear-view mirror: a crucifix on a chain and Frosty the
Snowman with red earmuffs, black gloves and a flat-brimmed
black Spanish hat, a *sombrero cordobés*. I hoped their magic
worked.

   On the outskirts of the small town of Magdalena, we
passed a group of pilgrims walking along the highway.
Penitentes, perhaps. They were gathering around a man who
stood on the elevated embankment of an irrigation canal,
holding up a large cross. For some strange reason I thought
about *Cabeza de Vaca*, the 16th- century Spanish explorer and
Florida ship-wreck survivor.[27] *Antonio Núñez Cabeza de Vaca*
was enslaved for part of his years-long sojourn along the
southern coast, living naked and half-starved. But he gradually
came to be regarded as a great faith-healer or medicine-man,
his reputation grew, and he was eventually followed around
by huge crowds of *indios*, who sought his healing
ministrations. I can't be sure, but I think he might have been
winging it—like I was, with my improvised rituals—relying on

the *placebo effect* to heal the ailing *indios,* since some of his customers actually got better. But great suffering sometimes brings great gifts, so maybe he really was a healer.

Finally, Cabeza de Vaca reconnected with some Spaniards after reaching the north Baja coast of the Gulf of California and returned to Spain. He wrote a long epistle to the King about his experiences among the aboriginal inhabitants between Florida and the Gulf.
Maybe Cabeza de Vaca passed through the area near Caborca during his harrowing adventures.

Some of the worshippers Antonio, Armando and I passed were already kneeling in front of the 2 x 4 cross. Yes, this was Good Friday, an appropriate day for my journey. Antonio told me about a famous wooden statue of St. Francis in Magdalena. It was said to have curative powers for those whose faith was strong enough. If you had a cousin who was sick, for example, you could pray to the statue and promise that, if he or she was cured, you would carry out some difficult deed. It was regarded as a serious matter to make such a promise and fail to carry it out. I made a mental note of that and thought about my own promise to return to Caborca.

Armando got off at Magdalena. We shook hands and he wished me well: *"Que le vaya bien."* May it go well with you. Antonio and I drove on towards Santa Ana, where Highway 2 branches off west to Caborca. At the main intersection of the two highways, I was shocked to see and recognize the same filling station where Phil and I had stopped for gas before crossing the desert! This was the last place I had been relatively conscious before the accident. Why was I so excited to find this confirmation of my dim memory image? Perhaps it was simply that, with this recognition, I was finally, after so many years, re-entering the sacred precincts of my initiation. We stopped at a taxi stand—a car parked in front of a bar— and I haggled with another driver for a ride from here to Caborca. This time it was going to cost me sixty bucks. What am I going to do, walk? *"¡Adelante!"* Onward! Let's get out of here! Just get me to Caborca!

El Camino de las Crucitas

FEDERAL HIGHWAY 2, FROM SANTA ANA THROUGH CABORCA to Sonoyta, is an eye-opener of a highway. I soon began to notice small crosses and shrines along the roadside where people had died. For this holiday weekend there were Red Cross ambulances stationed every few miles, and police cars parked next to trailered displays of demolished vehicles, with dummies hanging out the windows, red paint splashed all over, and large, hand-painted signs saying: *"La imprudencia."* I'll let you translate. This was indeed a very dangerous highway. In my mind, I re-named it, *"El Camino de las crucitas," The* road of little crosses. A less euphemistic name would have been "blood alley." My new driver, Joel, pronounced ho-él, assured me there were many accidents along this particular stretch: He himself had hit a pig one night, totaling his car and injuring his leg in the process. The pig died. The road consists of two lanes of asphalt, straight and narrow, built on an elevated roadbed because of flash floods. There is no shoulder. As I already said above, if you leave the asphalt, you roll. There is heavy traffic in both directions, and lots of eighteen-wheeler trucks.

Highway 2 is the only highway connecting all of Baja California with the rest of Mexico. It is a main artery, soaked in blood.

As we approached Pitiquito, I had another shock of recognition. We were passing *the same railroad crossing* where I awoke long enough to tell Phil to slow down. I was certain of it and, as it turned out, this was the only such crossing between Santa Ana and Caborca. We were now within two kilometers of my destination. We drove up a rise, through the village of Pitiquito, and down onto the broad desert plain over which lay sprawling the long-feared, long-awaited town of Caborca, Sonora, México.

La Pobreza

ONE THING MY GUIDEBOOKS AND MEMORIES HAD NOT prepared me for was the shock of Mexico's poverty compared to our relative wealth in the U.S. I had forgotten about the grim conditions in which many are forced to live, in a nation where the gulf between rich and poor is old and deep. In the United States poverty is somewhat ghettoized, but in Mexico it is generally and abundantly visible. By the time I arrived in Caborca I was in a state of shock. The combination of a lack of sleep, my mother's death the day before, the arduous connections, the uncertainty of travel and circumstances, the anticipation of my return to Caborca, plus the emotional assault of widespread poverty, *la pobreza,* in plain view, made for an altogether harrowing journey. Added to that was the language barrier. For all my apparent fluency, my comprehension was actually poorer than I had expected, running at a measley 50-60 per cent, barely enough to catch the drift of what was being said. Fatigue didn't help, of course, but still . . .

I checked into a motel, paid the driver, walked to my room, closed the door and fell onto the bed. What a trip! I lay resting for a while, but was too keyed up to sleep. My mind was racing. There was much to do, much to prepare. So far so good, Paco. You made it! I looked at the cross, still wrapped in its shroud, leaning against the wall, wondering where, when and how I would assemble and "plant" it.

It's funny how that verb wants to be used, *to plant,* as if the wood of the cross were still alive, and the cross, once planted, would start to root and ramify and exfoliate and blossom and bear fruit. I suppose that's how it is with a cross. You plant it to mark a place of death, and then something grows out of that death. I wondered how much the interwoven mythologies of Dionysus, Christ and other young, dying gods had fed into that ancient mythologem of life growing out of death. Both were conceived of as young, murdered or dismembered gods, the transformative energies of the vine, the spiritual ecstasies inherent in the grape, changed from grape juice into wine.

I wanted to hole up in my room, to rest and avoid any more stress, if only the linguistic kind, but I knew I couldn't afford that luxury. I made a list of things to ask the motel manager, not knowing what I would need: car rentals? taxis? fresh batteries? film? food? money exchange?

The manager's name was Umberto, a pleasant man with dark curly hair, glasses and a moustache. He was patient and helpful. I showed him my list of questions and soon we were discussing my mission. He asked to see the photo I had brought. To my surprise he recognized a few of the people in the photo, or their signatures on the back, and began looking up their names in the phone book. Then he was dialing the phone and talking to someone! Am I prepared for this? "Hell, no," I said to myself. Whereupon Umberto informed me that some members of the Red Cross would be over to pick me up shortly. What!? He had telephoned the Red Cross office and *they were waiting for me*! How could that be? Ah, the letter I had written and sent two weeks earlier. They got it! The reality of all this was moving fast! I hadn't slept the night before, hadn't eaten anything since my too-early breakfast, was feeling woozy, and had just barely arrived in Caborca. So, I went into the dining room to wait for the Red Cross contingent to show up. I eased into the local cuisine with *sopa de ajo*, garlic soup once again, recommended as an effective proof against the dreaded stomach troubles known as *turista,* aka *Montezuma's Revenge*.

La Cruz Roja de Caborca

HALFWAY THROUGH MY GARLIC SOUP I LOOKED UP AND SAW three men advancing toward me across the room, two in khaki uniforms and one in a yellow windbreaker and red baseball hat. I stood and introduced myself to them. The men in uniform were Gustavo—the Comandante of the Cruz Roja—and his young assistant, whose name I didn't catch. The third man was one of the ambulance drivers from the photograph, Carlos Pino, whose youthful image and autograph I had been carrying for nearly twenty-eight years! This was a powerful moment

134

indeed. We shook hands, grinned, gaped and chatted. I hauled out the famous photo and we studied it. After a while Gustavo said they had some business to take care of and would return when I had finished my meal. Then we would all drive to the Cruz Roja headquarters where we could plot our strategy for the ceremony of the cross. We shook hands again and said good-bye, all of us moved by the momentousness of the meeting. They whirled on their heels and marched out of the restaurant, leaving me in a daze with my garlic soup, tortilla and refried beans. Standard, simple fare in a Mexican desert town. The tortillas and beans were unsurpassable.

An hour later someone knocked on the door to my motel room. This time an interpreter had accompanied the Red Cross members, a godsend for me, since my Spanish was good enough to get me into trouble, but not always good enough to get me out again. The interpreter, Manuel González, was fluent in English, having studied at the University of Tennessee and the University of Arizona. He was a professor of philosophy and sociology at the University of Sonora in Caborca. For twelve years he had been donating his services to the Cruz Roja, much of which involves helping Americans in need of emergency medical treatment (the highway!), legal and other kinds of help. Manuel listened to my Spanish for a minute, then said I wouldn't have any trouble. (There's the problem: I sound fluent, but I'm not. I've forgotten too much!) We all piled into a white Chevy Suburban and drove to their headquarters.

As we walked toward the Comandante's office, Gustavo pointed out my letter, prominently displayed on a glass partition. They were proud of it. Two more men from the photo, Billy Ortega and Leonardo Elias Jaime, both tall and good-looking, were waiting for us. Counting Carlos Pino, there were now *three men from 1963* gathered for this unusual reunion. No one could remember anything about my accident, nor were there any *archivos*, or records, on file. So many years, so many wrecks, so many emergencies in the middle of the night. They wanted to know if my friend, *Felipe*, was OK. (He's fine, married with children, living in California.) Or if the government had given me any disability money. (*Nada*. Nothing.)

When I told them that my mother had just been killed and that I wanted to read a poem in her memory when we planted the cross, there was a palpable change of atmosphere in the small room. Words were suddenly difficult. Had I said something to offend somebody? Gustavo had a strained look on his face and stood with his back to the wall, staring across the table at a row of books. Billy started to guffaw. Carlos was silent.

Then I realized that, for these men, crying in public was a great embarrassment, and nothing would so readily dispose them to cry as the loss of a mother. I had forgotten about that aspect of Latin culture that requires a man to dominate certain emotions. I quickly changed the subject and made a joke to ease the tension. The meeting broke up shortly thereafter, and we all agreed to convene at eleven the next morning. They would drive me to a spot "ten miles west of Caborca," Phil's estimate of the approximate site of the collision. By Manuel's calculations that would be 16 kilometers or so.

That night I wrote a letter of thanks to the Cruz Roja ambulance drivers. It was a laudatory speech, a song of praise for these anonymous men who volunteer their time and lives to help people in crisis. Most of them work without pay, under conditions that would surely intimidate lesser souls. The more time I spent with them, the more grateful I was, not only for whatever role they might have played in my own rescue twenty-eight years earlier, but also simply for what they do day after day, year after year. I tried to convey those sentiments in the rough draft I wrote before retiring. There would be time to finish it in the morning.

I woke to a distant rooster calling forth a clear, warm day, good for a ceremony in the desert. At breakfast I worked on the speech, occasionally stopping my puzzled young waiter, Mario, to ask his opinion of verbs and nouns about which I was doubtful. He was cautious at first, but then expanded into his new role of walking grammarian, with increasing pride. Verbs-on-the-hoof! Flying conjugations! Side-order syntax!

What an interesting way to work through the breakfast shift!

At eleven o'clock Manuel the interpreter picked me up and we drove to the Cruz Roja office. Manuel had brought an army camp-shovel and his own small tape recorder with a blank cassette, so we would have something to dig with and a way of recording the speeches for posterity. At the headquarters we all greeted each other, took a few photographs and stood around chatting. We compared the present building to the one in my photograph. An addition had been built onto the front, obscuring what had been the original exterior window. I walked inside and noticed the same window now behind a counter in an interior reception room, my letter in Spanish still taped to it. Back outside and more conversation. Apparently, we were waiting for someone. Finally, everyone was ready. We got into two vans—*los Chevy Subúrban*—and took off. I sat between Carlos Pino, who still had his baseball hat, and Manuel. I had brought my camera, notebook and the cross, no longer enshrouded in black plastic and tape, but assembled and gleaming white. Manuel complained to Gustavo about the exhaust fumes engulfing the cab from a hole in the Chevy's floor, alerting him that if he didn't open a window, we would all be dead by the time we arrived! Gustavo grinned and cranked down the window. Whew! That's better!

Now we were on our way, rolling over the same road where I had met my fate. I couldn't possibly know where the accident had actually occurred, but my body was tense and alert. I asked Manuel about the Spanish names for the different varieties of cactus in the area: *el ocotillo, el saguaro, la cholla, el pitayo.* We looked at the ragged gullies alongside the elevated roadbed and I asked Manuel the Spanish word for "flash flood." He replied: *"Inundación."* Yes, of course. Inundation. That's what Noah got caught up in. That's what I got caught
up in, twenty-eight years ago. That's why I'm sitting here today, between Carlos and Manuel, breathing a mixture of equal parts carbon monoxide and fresh desert air, holding a cross and a camera, a buzzing in my guts from too much coffee, too little sleep, strange microbes and nerves.

In the distance, both ahead and behind us, ran a low mountain range spiked with saguaros like whiskers on a giant's jaw. The mountains serve to catch and precipitate precious moisture, flushing it through the arroyos and down into the water table where it slowly feeds the 2000-ft. deep wells of Caborca. The mountains also provide something for the sun to creep up to at dawn, a rocky backdrop to leap out from behind, like an Aztec god in battle array, dressed to kill, hurling itself in the end over the crenelated battlements of the western peaks. I could see why certain landscapes gave rise to particular myths. It was difficult for me not mythologize this landscape—sun and saguaros, mountains and mesquite, arroyos and *zopilotes*. Speaking of mythic landscapes, I had learned that this desert was where the Yaqui indians had lived, the culture that Carlos Castaneda wrote about in his famous "don Juan" books of the late 60s and early 70s. I could almost feel the shamanic aspects of the desert, imagine the peyote-fed, hallucinogenic states of mind that flourished here amidst the rocks, cacti and arroyos.

In the foreground ahead of us stood a large hillock, a volcanic intrusion known to geologists as a *monadnock*, a big rock sticking up out of the desert floor. I asked Manuel if that particular rock had a name. He paused, then said: "*La basura.*" Curious. That means "garbage" in English. I didn't ask him why they named it that, because I thought I knew. Besides, we were nearing the ten-mile mark. We slowed down as we approached the area, but there was no place to get off the road, so we drove ahead to the next available turn-out, a cattle gate. The grazing land was now fenced here, surely boosting the profit margins of the ranchers and reducing the workload of the Cruz Roja ambulance drivers in one stroke.

We parked under a tall mesquite bush for the meagre shade it afforded. I immediately began scouting for the "right spot," according to some ancient and intuitive sense of space, an act of personal geomancy. I noticed a permanent shrine with a cross and weathered wreath on our side of the road, a few yards back toward Caborca. Walking across to the north side of the highway and its west-bound lane, I found a spot directly opposite the shrine, off the roadway, slightly elevated, with a large circular open space about twelve feet in diameter, free of vegetation. I stood in the little clearing, looked across the highway and lined myself up with the concrete and terrazzo shrine. When I was directly parallel to it, I scuffed a spot in the dirt with my shoe. Manuel handed me the shovel and I started to dig a hole. He stopped me for a "ground-breaking" photograph, and I then proceeded to chip away at an obdurate aggregation of red dirt and splintered rocks. This was not going to be easy. The rocks resist the shovel, so you don't really dig per se; it's more like *prying* a hole into the ground. By the time I had pried a foot's worth of rocks out of the surrounding dirt, I had worked up a sweat. It was mid-day, around 75 degrees F. No clouds. I placed the sharpened-stake end of the cross in the hole and held it while Billy Ortega tapped on the top with a rock. Then he held it plumb while I backfilled it with dirt. I tamped the dirt with the shovel handle and my heel; then we all gathered surface rocks to place around the base of the cross to support it. We added more and more rocks until we had a fairly sturdy pyramid of about the right proportions to the height of the cross. I fussed with it a bit, adding a rock here and there for shape, profile and volume, the sculptor in me activated and in good form. Then I chinked some of the crevices with smaller, sharper stones for increased stability, the aboriginal engineer in me not wanting to be left out.

We stood back to look at the fruit of our efforts. Everyone was satisfied that it would stand for a while, that it was as stoutly planted as it was going to get. That's all I could ask. After all, this was not the Taj Mahal we were building, it was a moment in time that we were celebrating with two white sticks, a few rocks and some words. Manuel pulled out *his* tape recorder and began to speak into it. Suddenly he finished with his introduction and thrust the black box up to my face. Everybody waited for me to speak.

PART SIX
The Moment of Truth

El Momento de la Verdad

THE MOMENT OF TRUTH HAD ARRIVED. This was what I had been
anticipating for months and years. I took out my notes, we
tested the microphone to make sure the machine was
recording, and I began to speak. I recited the inscription
laminated to the cross, then the poem I had written for my
mother on the bus, and finally the speech praising the very
men who stood before me in a half-circle around the cross,
hands folded out of respect. I paused now and then as I
choked up, struggling with the lump in my throat. We all stood
there amidst the scruffy, spiny Sonoran chaparral, amidst the
pitayos and chollas and saguaros, seven sweating mammals
huddled over a cross, humans with beating hearts, dwarfed by
the immensity of the desert and the pitiless sky, driven here
by some deep instinctual need to perform this ceremony of
recognition, to acknowledge in some small way that we exist,
that we exist here, and that our existence is dependent on
forces beyond our comprehension and control. Our very
presence here today reveals a truth: that *much of what
matters in life consists in aligning ourselves deliberately with
that which we cannot comprehend*. This will always be true so
long as there is anything worthy of the title of "humanity" or
"culture." In the end, this *religious instinct* is what
distinguishes us from the other animals, our fellow creatures,
at least as much as does our language, our memory or our
opposable thumb. The animals, be it noted, never were
separated from their inherent instincts, the way and to the
degree we were. Thus the Latin etymology for the word
"religious" connotes a reconnection, a linking back—*re,*
"back," plus *ligare,* "to link, tie or connect"—i.e., to link back
or re-connect to something we came from, once knew or once

141

were. The animals, never having lost that link, are naturally "religious."

Paradoxically, that same religious sense which separates us from the animals also unites us with the animals, because only through this kind of human self-reflection and self-awareness can we see ourselves in proper perspective: protoplasmic bags of dreaming stardust hurtling through space, clinging to a cooling rock whose bounties and scarcities, blessings and terrors, origins and ends, we share with every other thing, animate and inanimate, for all time. Whatever we might think about "heaven," there is no other empirical world for us, and we must come to terms with what we are, who we are and where we are. As for the why of it, we can only speculate, imagine and dream.

Before departing from the cross, we paused for photographs, Manuel and I trading the photographer duties. Billy seemed impatient with all the posing and kept yelling at me to forget the *chingada* ("fucking") camera. I think he may have embarrassed his comrades with his rough-and-tumble invectives, but I was too immersed in the event to be bothered by anything.

Manuel and I walked back across the highway to look at the permanent shrine. It consisted of a concrete base with a large upright tablet, surmounted by a cast concrete cross. Molded onto the front surface of the tablet was the shape of an open book, with the name of the deceased embedded in black letters: "Higinio Juárez Suárez. Agosto, 22 de 1987. D.E.P." The initials, D.E.P., *Descanse en Paz*, are the Spanish equivalent of our saying, Rest In Peace, R.I.P. Affixed to the cross itself was a cast aluminum crucifix.

Several desiccated flower wreaths lay against the shrine. It had been erected as a memorial, perhaps by the wife or parent of the deceased. I thought about the cemeteries I had seen in Italy, and the one in Caborca I had passed on the way into town. Much attention is lavished on gravesites and shrines in these old-world cemeteries, in comparison to which ours sometimes look more like places of forgetting than of remembering. For these people life after death is a tangible reality, the ancient tradition of *ancestor worship* alive and well, and *memory of the dead a vital part of life.*

I paid my respects to this companion in death and memory, then Manuel and I trudged through the brush and gathering heat to the waiting *Subúrban*. On the drive back to Caborca, I felt a great sense of satisfaction and accomplishment, as if I had just completed an immense task, which in a sense I had.

Within a few miles of the ceremony site we passed a group of huts and a ramshackle building forming a small compound. I had the impression it was both living quarters and a store of sorts. Manuel said you could buy a Coke there. He didn't say what else. There were chicken-wire pens for goats or chickens. As I looked at it, I felt a creeping feeling of recognition. This had to be the place where Phil pulled over immediately after the accident, shouting "*Médico, médico!*" to the poor sleeping occupants. (I assume they'd been asleep.) I asked Manuel if he knew anything about it. He said it was called *"Patas locas."* Crazy hooves or crazy paws. I didn't want to stop the caravan to go exploring this lead. We had done enough for now. I wrote down the name in my notebook, memorized what I could of the place as it dwindled into the receding desert behind us. Someday I would try to ask Phil White about it, to see if his memories matched what I had just seen.

Gustavo said he would make a copy of the ceremony cassette-tape for me, so we returned to the Cruz Roja headquarters, the atmosphere now casual and friendly. The weather was beautiful. I joked about why Carlos Pino was in the front row of the photograph. Was it because he was the *jefe*, the boss, or because he was so handsome? The others hesitated, then got the joke and seized the opportunity to launch a barrage of insults at Carlos, who grinned happily at being the object of so much attention. More photographs, conversations, philosophizing. Leonardo told me that they had talked the night before about my arrival there, about how impressed they were, and honored, that someone would bother to come from so far away, and after so many years, to pay his respects to them. They were touched and moved by it. As we talked further, I told him that I would be going to the cathedral later on to light a candle for my mother. He wanted to know what church I belonged to, and I could tell from his manner that he had no frame of reference by which to understand the fact that I had no church, that I was carrying out this action strictly on my own, that I was operating, as I said earlier with the cow-skull burial, *extra ecclesiam*. Finally, I told him that I had been raised Protestant but that I had a great appreciation for some of the Catholic traditions. This was true and seemed to satisfy him. I could tell that his religion was very important to him, that it gave him everything he needed to make sense of his life and to comport himself with dignity in the face of whatever circumstances he might encounter.

As people came and went, my conversation shifted from one person to another. Soon Carlos Pino and I were discussing once again the details of the accident, and he offered an interesting theory about what had happened that night. He was hesitant at first, apparently unsure of his idea. But the more he talked the more confident he became that he had discovered the truth, until finally his face glowed with a certainty born of recognition. He announced to me that, when Phil's car hit the cow, it was the *horn of the cow* that had pierced my eye. I was amazed, not by the possibility that this had happened, but by his *certitude* in the absence of knowledge, and by the *satisfaction* he gained from it. It was as if the fantasy-image of a horn penetrating an eye satisfied the criteria of an imaginal, archetypal category in the mind of Carlos Pino, to such an extent that his body responded by telling him this was "truth." Such a certainty functions independently of the "objective facts." No one will ever know with objective certainty what happened that night. But for Carlos Pino the image of the loss of an eye by means of a *cornada*, a goring, satisfied his requirements for a mythic understanding of a profound event. To some extent Carlos' image was probably his own personal or cultural projection onto someone else's experience, but it could also be an archetypal fantasy with potential relevance for myself and others as well. But I am grateful to Carlos for his sincerity. The image came to him unbidden, like water gushing from a hidden spring or a rabbit leaping from a bush, a manifestation of the spontaneous mythopoetic activity of the psyche. This

144

mythologizing process is an ever-present possibility in each of us and, though it is damned by rationalists as mere superstition, I believe it is ultimately vital to the well-being of both individuals and cultures.

When it all came to an end, Gustavo presented me with the tape and we all shook hands yet again, exchanging thanks and good wishes. They invited me to come back any time: I would always be welcome. I replied that maybe next time I could buy them all *una cerveza*, and Billy, who already had a beer-belly on him—*una barriga*—piped up, saying: *"¡O dos!"* Or two! We all laughed, waved, and Manuel drove me back to my room.

By now I had accomplished most of my mission. I had gotten to Caborca, no small feat in itself. I had met some of the people in the photograph; traveled "about ten miles west" of the town; planted the cross; and recited the poems. I had not met the pilot of the crop-duster or found out his last name (*José* was all I knew); I had not seen the hospital or met the doctor; and I had not yet gone to the Cathedral to light a candle and say a prayer both for the soul of my mother, and out of my own gratitude for the gifts I had received.

Manuel was extremely generous and helpful throughout, placing himself at my disposal for whatever I might need, which, at the moment, was rest. Later on, I wanted to go to the Cathedral. He would be glad to pick me up at 4:00 PM. I was thirsty, so before retiring I stopped in for a Coke at the restaurant. I thought that would be safe to drink. The waiter served it in a glass, over ice. The ice may have been a mistake, but I wouldn't know about it for several hours. In retrospect, I should have ordered a beer.

In the afternoon Manuel arrived on time and we drove directly to a bustling *super-mercado* where I found several items I needed: a new notebook, Spanish comic books and a toy for my son, and some candles in water glasses with images of the Virgin stenciled on the outside. I would light one for my mother at the cathedral. The others I would bring home as souvenirs and gifts.

From the market we drove past the *zócalo,* or main plaza, to the cathedral, which the locals refer to as *La Candelaria.* We walked into the church and I was surprised to find myself responding with a strong emotion. I had been functioning in a daze, negotiating the various stages of my complicated journey; but powerful emotions were just beneath the surface: I had not really had a chance to grieve. Now, entering the sanctuary of the church, feeling the immensity of its interior space, and confronting the beauty of the sacred figures adorning the walls, I felt a wave of emotion in a moment of release.

We approached the front of the church and Manuel waited as I walked to the chapel on the left. I lighted my candle and added it to the others. The moment I knelt before the altar, a rush of tears took me and I sobbed silently for several minutes. Finally, I was in a place where I could release some of these emotions—an amazing mixture of pain, sadness and grief, plus an astounding joy and gratitude, something I had felt briefly on the bus ride to the border. Though drenched with grief, I was glad to experience what was happening.

When I was finally able, I lifted my head. Above me was a life-sized crucifix, a standing Christ, a Madonna-and-Child and, slightly to my left, the Virgin Mary, her face a picture of solicitous concern, her eyes fixed directly on mine. Perfect. The precise placement of this elevated divine figure, and the direction of its gaze, offered eloquent testimony as to the meaning and purpose of the divine persons, equivalent to twenty volumes of theology. Anyone with a human heart will instinctively understand this living symbolism of the Holy Mother of God directly addressing the personal concerns of the supplicant—apart from all postures of belief or disbelief or doctrine.

And for me, that afternoon, the very act of kneeling, of genuflection before the divine figures, was sufficient to release the emotions essential to healing. I did not want to throw myself at the feet of the priest and convert to Catholicism, or any other religion, but I felt very deeply the value of an intact religious tradition to those for whom it still constitutes an effective *container* or *vessel*. I was grateful on this day to be able to find this sanctuary in which to be with my grief, to be with the emotions in a way that would not disturb, frighten or embarrass anyone. At last I stood up, dried my eyes and blew my nose. I lingered a brief moment longer, then turned and left. Manuel was waiting for me.

The rest of the day unfurled slowly. It was a holiday, and warm. We drove to the seventeenth-century adobe mission, begun by the Jesuits but completed by the Franciscans. Manuel explained that the plaza in front of the mission was the site of a famous battle in 1857, from which Caborca takes its full name: *Heróica Caborca.* Heroic Caborca. The Mexican government had been in disarray at the time, so an opportunistic American lawyer from California named "General" Henry Crabb decided to meddle in Mexican politics. Maybe he could take over Sonora and get rich in the process. He rode with a group of soldiers called the "Filibusterers" into Caborca and tried to take the town. They were repulsed by the citizens and Crabb was killed in the battle. The date of the battle was April 6, now an upcoming day of celebration for the people of Caborca. I missed it by a week.

Before returning to the motel, Manuel showed me his office at the University of Sonora campus in Caborca, and took me home to meet his lovely wife, Addy, and their two children. They served me tea and cookies and we talked around the kitchen table while the boys played outside. Finally, it came time to leave and I felt like I was leaving friends. On the way to the motel we stopped by the hospital where I had been treated after the accident. Like the Red Cross, this too had been enlarged since 1963, but at the rear we found the original building. He said in those days it was a four- or five-bed hospital. I could see which room I had been in. The whole unit was now used for *urgencias*, emergencies. Since it was late, and the place seemed deserted, we didn't try to go in. It was enough to have seen it. We drove slowly back to the motel, and as we said good-bye, Manuel told me: "I have a feeling we will meet again."

After dinner, I retired to my room to prepare for my return to Tucson. I had originally planned to spend more time in Caborca, but due to uncertainties regarding the date of my mother's funeral, I knew it would be best to return to Tucson. I would take the early morning bus, *la diaria*, originating daily from Caborca, in the hope that it wouldn't be too crowded on

Easter morning. The bus was supposed to leave at 5:30 AM and I had to arrive early enough to get a ticket. I arranged for a wake-up call at 4:30 AM.

Since getting back to the states promised to be an ordeal no matter how or when I did it, I might as well get it over with. I laid out what I would need in the morning, showered and lay down to rest. I was feeling ill with the first stirrings of a cold and a bolt of *turista* churning my insides like a great mill. Was it the ice cubes? Or the dinner meal? No matter. Dig out the indigestion tablets and go to sleep, or rather, good luck trying to sleep. Whether it was my intestinal discomfort or the meal, the strain of what I'd been through or the anticipation of what lay ahead, my body refused to sleep. Try as I might, I could only manage a dull slumber all night long. I lay in bed, turning frequently, aware of the nearly constant droning of heavy truck traffic along "the highway." Truck after truck hauling goods across the desert. My prayers were with the drivers for safe journeys all.

Adiós, Caborca

AT 4:15 AM I GAVE UP TRYING TO SLEEP, rose, showered and called for a taxi. By 5:00 AM I stood in front of the bus station, visible from the road. It was a long wall with a single door in it. A few cars idled in front, discharging passengers. I paid the taxi driver and walked through the door. Good Lord! It was packed with people! Once again, I was the only blue-eyed creature in the room and to these folks I must have seemed very exotic. Every head turned when I walked in. (After a while you get used to being conspicuous.)

I looked around and saw no information sign regarding tickets, so I asked a man where I could buy one. He said there weren't any. What? They're all sold out, he said. Oh boy, now what? He sized me up for a moment and said that his daughter had an extra ticket for her girlfriend, and if she didn't show up, I could buy the extra ticket from her. Well, there's a chance, at least. How much would the ticket cost? *"Once mil pesos."* Eleven thousand pesos. In those days, that was a few dollars. I looked at the clock. 5:10 AM. Nothing to do but wait and see if I would have any luck.

Araiza

THE MAN I WAS TALKING TO APPEARED TO BE IN HIS 50'S, silver-haired and dignified. He wore clean khakis and had the air of a successful farmer, a man of distinction. Perhaps a manager or owner of something. I was half-crazed with lack of sleep, plummeting health and barely able to speak—let alone Spanish—so early in the morning. I was hanging on by a thread, so I didn't get his name. He was here with his wife to see his daughter off on the bus. The daughter worked in Tucson. *"Mojada,"* he said with a wink. That means wet or soaked. At first, I didn't understand, then I realized he meant she was a "wetback," working illegally in the United States. Well, whatever it takes to survive, I thought. Caborca was typical of many so-called Third World areas where poverty is rampant and wealth highly concentrated in the hands of a few. And the wealthy don't gladly relinquish their control over that wealth. The Mexican Revolution was supposed to change all that, as was the Russian Revolution. But something in human beings seeks to satisfy self-interest. Christians call it "sin" or the temptations of the Devil—the "ruler of this world." I prefer to think of it as "instinct." Human society will always be a fitful balance between behaviors based on the instinctual demand for self- preservation and behaviors based on the cultural or spiritual demand for the sacrifice or the *modification of instinct*. The dance this young woman goes through each time she crosses the border at Nogales is a direct result of the cultural dilemma. Should she obey the letter of the law, or help to support her family? Which is more important?

In the course of my conversation with the man I told him why I was in Caborca. I also mentioned in passing that a crop-duster pilot named José had flown me to Nogales, but that I hadn't found out his last name.

149

Without hesitation the gentleman said: *"Araiza."* I was startled. Was he telling me the pilot's last name? Yes, he was. José and Jesús Araiza were two brothers who flew the crop-dusting plane—the *avión fumigador*—in those days. He'd known them both. I wrote the names in my notebook and asked if they were still alive. He said they had both died, José about five years ago. *This piece of information, so crucial to me, came from the one stranger I approached at random in the crowded Caborca bus station at five o'clock in the morning on an Easter Sunday.* I realize that Caborca, for all practical purposes, functions like any small town, and that there must be extensive, intricate relations among its inhabitants. Therefore, it was not an astronomically improbable coincidence, not a flat-out miracle, that he should have known the name of the pilot who, *twenty-eight years ago*, had airlifted me out of Caborca. Nevertheless, it is significant to me that, in a roomful of strangers, the one person I approached at random, without forethought, just happened to carry that information, and it added to my sense that some transpersonal power was "guiding" me throughout the process.

The bus was late, and the crowd swelled by the minute. This was going to be tight. I had finally become invisible in the room. The fact that I was speaking Spanish to the well-known local man, rather than English or Tibetan or Urdu, may have helped the locals accept my presence after my shocking entry into their midst. I waded through the crowd to position myself for whatever was going to happen when the bus arrived. My friend the gentleman had taken an interest in my adventure and carried the suitcase for me. He told me that I could pay the driver and ride the bus without a ticket, but I would have to stand up the whole way! I found his daughter in the crowded loading area and asked if her friend had shown up. At least that's what I thought I said. She nodded. At least I thought she did.

When the bus finally arrived and the driver opened the door, the entire crowd ganged toward the narrow opening in a ballet of courteous ruthlessness. Everyone jostled for position and advantage, but there was no shouting or complaining. Everyone was urgent but quiet. We were packed shoulder-to-shoulder like cattle at a loading gate. All the surging back and forth reminded me of the crowds at English soccer matches—but without the English riots. What seemed to determine the order in which people actually boarded the vehicle, were the elbows. *Coude majeure*! Elbow rule! If, in the crush of bodies, I could get my elbow wedged in front of someone else's arm, I went first. But if the other person managed to get his or her elbow in front of me, then I had to yield. To overrule an elbow would have been cause for dispute!

To my surprise, just before the girl stepped onto the bus she turned around, reached out and said: *"Aquí!"* Here! She was handing me her extra ticket! Whoa! I thought her girlfriend had showed up and I would be standing the whole way. Apparently, we had miscommunicated a few minutes earlier. *O felix culpa!* I gave her a wad of eleven thousand pesos and she disappeared into the bus. A few elbows later I too was struggling up the steps with my bags. The farmer-father-friend was waving to me from outside the bus, wishing me well. I waved back and gave my ticket to the driver. *Número once*—seat number eleven. I heaved my suitcase onto the overhead rack and sat next to a quiet young man who gave no indication of wanting to talk. Fine with me.

Meanwhile the bus filled up with ticketed and unticketed passengers until all the benches and the entire aisle were jammed with bodies. Someone was using my shoulder as a backrest and my armrest as a seat. Another person used my left knee as a brace—or were they sitting on it? I was trapped and half-crushed, but at least I had a seat. No one seemed disturbed or surprised at having to stand, or at the crush of bodies.

An old campesino across the aisle lighted up a cigarette. Oh oh, I hate cigarette smoke. It makes me car-sick, and I'm already sick. Maybe the human wall in the aisle will block the smoke.

At 6:00 AM we were ready to leave. The driver engaged reverse gear with a prolonged metallic grinding as though the clutch disk was arguing with the flywheel. With a heavy clunk the spinning cog finally crunched into position and we backed out of the loading area. More sustained grinding and crunching and we managed to engage a forward gear. We crept over bumps and potholes to the edge of the famous highway. I hoped the driver had a large family and a positive outlook on life. Gustavo had shown me photographs at the Cruz Roja headquarters of a bus that had rolled, out on Highway 2. The driver had fallen asleep at the wheel. The roof of the bus was flattened to the tops of the seats. Bodies were laid out amidst stretchers and splints, blood-stains and bandages. One photo showed the interior. How did they get the passengers out? I asked Gustavo. He said they used a crowbar.

Once underway my seatmate fell asleep against the window. Lucky guy! Who can sleep? The driver labored through the four-speed gearbox in a slow facsimile of the mechanics of forward motion. The roads around here are rough on suspension, and it felt like the shock absorbers on our bus had used up their *élan vital* many miles ago. They felt like rigid steel struts, transmitting with mechanical fidelity every nuance of the road surface, through the stiff chassis to the rigid, red-vinyl seats, and from there all the way up the spinal column to the wobbly cranium and jiggling brain of every passenger on board this venerable *autobús*. I'm not complaining, just observing the conditions in which I find myself on this holy Day of Resurrection and Light.

Easter Sunrise

SPEAKING OF WHICH, THE SUN WOULD BE COMING UP SHORTLY. The stars had finished their tinkling praeludium, like glimmering silver bells, now muffled in black velvet slowly fading to blue. A solar overture was sounding off-stage, behind the mountains, announcing the major theme of today's symphony. Today the theme, like every other day since the formation of the planet, would be "The Return of the Light." How many times has the entire world awaited the latest, the ninety-eight-septillionth, variation on this theme? For how many millennia have creatures paused in their grazing or hunting or mating—

152

whatever they do at dawn—to mark the sacred moment and so participate in the immense majesty of this celestial music? How many generations of humans have awaited this moment?

For my part, I sat waiting for the sunrise, squirming on my seat to find the least damaging position, and I looked around the bus. The headliner up front was upholstered in Texas-brown Naugahyde done up in big diamond pleats. Two loudspeakers were screwed in place on either side, facing the passengers. The driver flipped a switch and a blend of salsa music and static came blasting out of the speakers like mulch from a shredder. The bouncy music added spice to the groaning bass continuo of the bus's drive train, the alto howling of the tires and the counter-rhythmic percussion of the rattling windows. The front windshield was cracked and dirty. Hanging from the rear-view mirror were two angora dice, two crucifixes and a baby shoe—more good luck charms. No Frosty the Snowman this time.

On the driver's visor a sign admonished, in English: "Let me see you smile." On the opposite visor tiny green and red lights glowed in the pre-dawn darkness. At first, I thought they were indicator lights of some sort, but it turned out they were part of a battery-operated crucifix. The lights were embedded in the cross itself, which in turn was mounted on a small wooden box concealing the battery. The cross glowed and winked like a swarm of fireflies as we ploughed through the desert. The driver carried on a long conversation with a man in front, but he kept his eyes on the road.

My eye was on the rim of the mountains ahead and the crescendo of light giving away the position of the hidden, soon-to-be-revealed sun. The mountains caught fire as the blazing corona slipped above the horizon, and the sun—ever-generous—once again scattered its regal light upon the waiting plains like an Aztec prince dressed in gold. And just as I wrote earlier, the self-same army of ancient saguaros, His Majesty's loyal retainers, were still standing at attention on the fields and slopes of Sonora, always ready to receive the ritual outpouring of their god. And in a sudden gesture of unanimity, they all hailed their leader in a stumpy, simultaneous salute. Just as suddenly, the dust particles on our windshield ignited brilliantly in the rays of the rising sun, and the crack in the glass gleamed like a sliver of mercury. The crack resembled a crazy grin on the face of our metal wagon, this behemoth rushing across the desert toward the returning king. I looked at my watch. It was 6:22 AM. At 6:23 we rolled into the village of Altar.

Something greedy in me might have hoped for an Easter sunrise circumstance more glamorous than this: this crowded bus rolling down the road a kilometer short of nowhere, this aching stomach of mine, this dizzy head, this dirty windshield and cacophony of noise. Something greedy would have chosen harps and organs, swans and Roman candles, roaring falls and mists and rainbows. But as I marked the event in memory I knew that this greedy part was not up to the moment. There was a better part in me that knew full well the value and meaning of the place and time of *this sunrise*. To the better part this was a fine moment indeed, truly an occasion for joy. *I knew I would never experience another Easter sunrise like it!*

We drove past fields and huts and I watched the eerie beauty of morning steam rising from a glistening canal. The farmers were irrigating their crops, getting a jump on the sun. Grape vines and pastures prevailed where there was water, scruffy chaparral where there was not. We stopped periodically to unload and load passengers, our bus like a biblical Leviathan wallowing through the desert sea, beaching in the occasional villages, spewing out its cargo like so many Jonahs, swallowing still more souls before plunging back into the deep. My seat companion slept the whole way. My backrest and knee companions got off at Magdalena. The back of my seat was not a comfortable place to rest my head, so instead I sat upright with my eyes closed, nodding the last hour to Nogales, still trying to sleep, trying to balance my head on top of my neck like an orange on the end of a stick, balanced, so that it wouldn't fall off if I did fall asleep. Once in a while the orange would start to fall off the stick and I would wake up. How much longer to Nogales?

At the outskirts of the city, large and forbidding factories squatted like fortresses behind high-security fences. These

154

were assembly plants—*maquiladoras*—owned by American companies but located just across the border to take advantage of the pool of cheap labor. It creates jobs for the Mexicans, but at what cost, I wondered, to their traditional way of life? Soon the factories gave way to smaller businesses and houses and we were in downtown Nogales.

Once off the bus I headed directly for the border. The bored customs guard looked at me with surprise and asked where I'd been. "Caborca," I replied, expecting a search of my suitcase. He asked where I lived. I told him. "OK," he said. That was it. I tried to drag my suitcase through the three-pronged turnstile, but it got caught and I had to clamber through one leg at a time, yanking at the recalcitrant bag. Now I was back in the States.

Remember, I hadn't really slept all night, again, and I hadn't eaten yet and had intestinal trouble to boot. I extricated myself from the turnstile and walked with as much dignity as I could muster, from the customs office to the Greyhound bus terminal. Another leg of the journey completed!

I sat in the Greyhound waiting room while the sounds of spoken Spanish enveloped me like an acoustic balm. Such a beautiful language. An hour later we were on our way. I wanted no conversations this time, just sleep, so for two hours I tried to balance the orange on the end of the stick. No luck.

By mid-afternoon—after more waiting on benches, hauling baggage, determining connections, digging for fares, talking to drivers and sitting in vehicles—I had reached the Tucson motel and could begin to relax. I was glad to be back in the States with a private room, a shower and a bed. Even as I unwound from the trip, however, I found that I didn't want to give up speaking Spanish. I pestered the maids in the hallway with contrived conversations in Spanish and ran into Eduardo the shuttle-driver in the restaurant. He recognized me and wanted to know how my trip went. I told him it was a hard trip, *un viaje muy duro*, but that I achieved my purpose or, as Manuel the interpreter put it, *cumplí mi promesa*. I fulfilled my promise. Maybe that's what the other pilgrims were doing on the highway outside of Madgalena, fulfilling promises made to their *santo*. When Eduardo asked me where I was off to next, I told him about my mother's death and the funeral I would be attending. He expressed his regrets with courteous phrases. We talked a bit longer, the Spanish coming easier to me than it had in Caborca. There was a good feeling between us. When Eduardo was called to the desk, he wished me luck and we shook hands. I finished my meal, then went back to the room and dictated some notes into my own pocket recorder.

The following day I stayed in bed. My cold had taken over control of the ship, and the circle of life now shrank to that rather small diameter afforded by a regimen of aspirin, liquids and bed rest. I was trying to gather enough strength to make it to Los Angeles the next day for my mother's funeral.

PART SEVEN
The Burial

El Entierro

IN THE MORNING THE MOTEL PALM TREES NEXT TO THE POOL rattled stiffly in a warm, dry wind. When I had arrived the first time, on my way to Mexico, the pool had been commandeered by young men from a nearby military base, but today only a body-builder was sitting by the pool, nursing along the tanning bulges of his most precious possession. The breakfast waitress, Mary, was an elderly Texas gal with down-home style and an amazing face—character wrinkles that wouldn't stop. She had a hard-boiled, mesquite-ranch manner, softened with a honey drawl and that hidden heart-of-gold that seems to flourish in the open-sky country of the Southwest. We joked about the miles she covered between the tables, all that exercise and the good shape she was in. It was time to leave. I called for a ride in the mini-van and we drove out to the Tucson airport.

Since I had some time before my flight, I got a shoeshine from a bow-legged blonde in red cowboy boots and jeans. She was open and friendly, and the airport was her corral and range. She loped back and forth in the wide, carpeted corridor roping "dogies" to shoeshine, roaming occasionally across the way to take or make personal calls on the payphone (no cellphones in those days). Judging from her arms, hands, legs, boots and athletic bearing, I guessed she was an old hand at coaxing and handling big animals.

The trip to Los Angeles and back to Tucson required four plane rides, four automobile rides, several hours of waiting in terminals, and, through it all, lots of emotion. My family had gathered at my mother's house before the funeral. Relatives from all over the country had arrived, many of whom I hadn't seen since childhood. My sister was out of the hospital, her arm in a cast and sling, her face bruised, arm and hand badly scraped but forming scabs at least. She was stiff, in pain and still in a daze. She was running on pure adrenalin. We held each other and cried for a while. There was very little to say. My favorite aunt joined us, and we all started bawling again. Once again, I had a huge lump in my throat, and I could barely swallow. Once in a while we would find something to laugh about, adding leavening to the density of sorrow. Finally, it came time to drive to the funeral home.

When we arrived, I saw more relatives from long ago and the tears would gush back up until the familiar lump lodged in my throat again. Maybe I should give the lump a name, like Fred or Oscar or Louie or something. My handkerchief—let's call him "Orlando"—was soggy. I sat between my sister and my aunt through the service. We had an entire box of Kleenex to share. We needed it. Miraculously, my mother's face was not badly cut, and the coroner found the body "suitable for viewing." When I saw her lying there for the first time I was racked by fresh fits of grief. The only other dead person I had ever seen was my father, lying in his casket, twenty-nine years earlier. I was so young then, uninitiated and uncomprehending, I don't think I ever achieved a state of true grieving, despite the tears I shed over his coffin and grave. This time I was older, and the difference in maturity and experience allowed more openness to and appreciation of the healing value of authentic grief. I found myself able to grieve not only the sudden passing of my mother, but, retroactively it seemed, the sudden passing of my father as well. And just as this death immediately prompted the image of a long-awaited reunion between my mother and my father, so it also prompted the image of a reunion between my father and me.

Earlier I referred to the emotions of joy and sorrow while riding on the bus from Tucson to Nogales, as I wrote the poem in Spanish for my mother; and then again when those same emotions came to visit me as I sat in the cathedral in Caborca. The joy came from a strong sense that my mother and father were reunited in some eternal part of the soul. To repeat: The insight in the last verse of the poem was that this was in fact their life-destiny, and that only upon my mother's death could this eternal aspect of their love be fulfilled.

158

This was a *joyful* image. It did not come to me by virtue of religious teaching, by the way, or by reasoning, or philosophy, but by virtue of my years of experience with dreams—and it came to me unbidden.

And in fact, over the years, my mother had told me of dreams she had had in which my father had appeared to her and said: "I'm waiting for you, honey." There was no doubt whatsoever in her mind, that, on some mysterious level of being, this was true. Nor did I have any reason to doubt the possibility. I don't know if her conviction was born of religious teachings, or if it came from the convincing reality of his appearance in her dreams. My guess is that it was a combination, but that the dreams had the edge over the teachings, since the dreams came from within her own deep experience.

I myself had also had a series of dreams over a period of years, in which my deceased father appeared, always with the feeling that it was *an objective image,* that is, a "visitation" of the deceased, rather than an image of my "father-complex," with which I was all too familiar. In other words, each dream in that series came to me convincingly. I always felt that I was actually seeing *the spirit of my deceased father,* coming into my dreams from "the other side," although I had *no particular beliefs* about the possibility of life after death. At any rate, I was only interested in *experience.* In one dream of my father, late in the series:

> *I find myself inside a coffin with my father. He is "dead." I inspect the hinges and interior of the coffin to make sure it is well-crafted. When I am satisfied, I reach over and squeeze his hand in a spontaneous gesture of affection. To my surprise I feel the slightest response from him. He is squeezing my hand in return! He is not dead after all. He is alive.* [End of dream.]

I do not want to "interpret" this dream. I am satisfied to have dreamed it and to be left with a certain feeling about death and the possibilities it veils and conveys. Dreams like

159

this can be gathered over time, enabling one to approach both life and death openly, with more anticipation and courage than a fearful, hesitant approach would allow. The ability to affirm *what is* should not be scoffed at, especially when the traditional affirmations of life and death through religious belief and practice, fall increasingly before the restless blade of our rational materialism and its haunted denial of the soul.

At the end of the funeral service, I waited as my mother's friends and relatives filed past the coffin. I didn't want to watch the procession. I sat there with the Kleenex box and my paper program, studying the wood-grain on the back of the pew in front of me—oak with a dark stain and semi-gloss varnish. Suddenly someone grabbed me and squeezed me in a bear hug, saying, "I love you." It was Phil White. I hadn't seen him in over twenty years. He had grown a beard, and the sensation of his whiskers bristling against my cheek and the stiff fabric of his suit under my hands provided a physical lattice for the crystallization of emotion. He said he would meet me outside, then turned and joined the procession.

When my turn came, I stood before the coffin, "viewing the body." I had forgotten the utter stillness that attaches to death. You look at the face, waiting for a flicker, and there is none. You look at the chest or abdomen, waiting for a breath, and there is none. I looked at my mother's face, whose features had been so familiar to me my entire life. Age and death had brought the underlying foundation of bones to the surface, offering a more structural sense of her face and, perhaps, who she was. I could see both more and less in that face. I appreciated the mortician's art that had given the slightest expression and blush of health to the abandoned tissues of her face, no longer quick and pulsing. There was humor in the expression, a wryness, an understanding, characteristics which she had possessed in life. One could have imagined that the mortician knew her. I said to myself, "They did a good job." I stood there for a long time. When I was ready to leave, I reached in the casket and touched her hand. It was cold. I said, "Good-bye, Mom," and walked out into the sun.

For the next hour or so I stood talking to relatives and friends from twenty, thirty and forty years back. Faces from the past floated up to me, bobbing in the light, every face intensely illuminated by the benevolent California sun. Brief conversations in a gentle tide of well-wishing, sympathy and sorrow. Handshakes and hugs. A childhood friend from my fifth and sixth years joined Phil and me. His name was Bill Kirk. He was a twin, one half of the configuration known to me in boyhood as "Bill-Bob Kirk." We started recalling memories, catching up on history, Bill now selling computers, his twin-brother Bob "running with the Indians in Dakota." Remember the day we ate the apricots before they were ripe because we couldn't wait, and were rewarded with indigestion for our impatience? And the "horny toads" we would catch under the grape vines, lift them by the horns and pet their bellies? And the time we snuck into Mr. Levy's goldfish pond in our bare feet? What about walking barefoot into the midst of the insidious "puncture weeds"? (I don't know the scientific name for these plants, but for a barefoot boyhood lived outdoors, "puncture weed" was scientific enough. They're called "goatheads" in New Mexico, where I live now.) What about the time we built a "sacred fire" in the back acre with dry grass and twigs, and the most important thing in the world was to keep that fire from going out? "Feed the fire! Feed the fire!" we yelled to one another in an ecstatic frenzy. It was the first time in our lives we felt truly responsible to a natural force beyond ourselves. A neighbor finally spotted us, and we got in trouble for it. But it was a heightened moment neither of us had forgotten.

When I mentioned it, Bill Kirk responded immediately: "Of course I remember the sacred fire!"

Patas Locas

IT WAS TIME TO LEAVE THE FUNERAL HOME. We all drove back to my mother's house for a meal and last visit. I met Phil's wife and children for the first time, then Bill Kirk joined us, and we stood outside talking. I told Phil I had just gotten back from my return trip to Caborca and pumped him for whatever memories he could dredge up. He confirmed my hunch about the huts called "Patas Locas" I had seen outside Caborca. That was indeed where we first stopped after the accident. He couldn't remember anything about how he found his way to the Red Cross or the hospital. He talked about his return from Caborca after the accident, after I had been flown out, how he drove straight through from Caborca to Southern California.

Understandably, he'd been still exhausted, and he fell asleep along the way, driving off the shoulder and rolling the VW. It landed upright, but with a flat tire. He changed the tire and kept driving. It was an eight-hour drive, all told. He didn't stop until he reached the hospital where I had been recovering from surgery.

We talked about our Spanish teacher, Mr. Allen, about the 30th high school reunion and the old high school gang. For a while, in high school, we used to get together, five or six of us classmates, and sing in harmony the popular Kingston Trio and Harry Belafonte Calypso songs. Phil and I were able to talk through the leftover concerns and urgencies, memories and facts, the loose ends of Caborca. At one point I embraced him, saying: "You saved my life."

The food was almost gone so we went inside and ate. More relatives and kind words, memories, shared biographies, connections re-weaving the fabric of the family after a crucial member has been torn out of it. Death is a powerful agent in human life, not only destroying and taking away, but giving new life and strength to what remains, like some great welder who tears down the family structure with a cutting torch, then gathers the sundered fragments, soaks them in an acid bath of grief, grinds each one down to bare metal to strip away all superfluities, then welds them all back together again to form a new and stronger whole. By the time I left the gathering, drove back to Ontario airport, flew to Los Angeles, flew to Tucson, caught a taxi to the motel and crawled into bed, I was feeling homogenized, pulverized, pasteurized, cauterized, mutilated, truncated, bifurcated, addled, saddled, bushed, shushed, crushed, shorn, torn, jogged, bogged, clogged, slogged, slugged, bugged, bashed, crashed, dashed, smashed, flashed, flooded, gutted, muddied, bloodied and wrecked.

Finally, I slept.

Final Twist

IN THE DAYS FOLLOWING THE FUNERAL I RESUMED my original itinerary through parts of the Southwest, which I had planned on continuing after my trip to Caborca—visiting friends in Santa Fe, attending a conference in Albuquerque. When the time finally came for my return flight home, the routing included another Los Angeles leg, for which I boarded a plane in Tucson. I had the aisle seat and a young man sat at the window. The middle seat between us was empty. I stashed my shoulder bag and strapped myself in. A few minutes later a flight attendant pulled the cabin door shut with a loud "clumph." We were ready for the push-back. The aircraft shivered slightly as the ground-mechanics on the low-slung pushback tractor attached the push-bar to the plane and began to engage the heavy bar. We moved a couple of inches. Soon we would be airborne.

Suddenly we stopped, the flight attendant re-opened the cabin door, and several late arrivals jostled aboard and hurried down the aisle. They settled near where I was sitting. Two women and a man. They were speaking English. The women sat in the two seats in front of me. The man squeezed into the middle seat next to me. Once settled, he leaned forward and said something in Spanish to the woman in front. *Mexicanos*, perhaps. Here was another opportunity to practice my Spanish—plus I was half-delirious with fatigue, illness and grief. So, I introduced myself to the man and we began to chat. When I told him where I had been in Mexico and what I had been doing there, his face changed, as if he were deep in thought or trying to make a decision. Then he turned to me and said, *"Mi hermana vive en México."* My sister lives in Mexico. I asked him, *"¿Dónde?"* Where? He replied, *"Caborca."*

163

PART EIGHT

The Paraclete of Caborca

WHILE IMMERSED IN THE EARLY STAGES OF WRITING about Caborca, I found an undated notation in my own handwriting, in a stack of papers. I could not recall where the statement had come from. The note simply said: "I am the Fool for Christ and the Paraclete of Caborca." I had jotted this down years earlier, long before it had occurred to me to return to Caborca, let alone write about my experiences there. Apparently, I had scribbled the enigmatic dictum on a piece of scratch paper. I assumed this was a dream fragment I had scribbled down and forgotten about. I vaguely remembered puzzling over it, feeling its uncanny quality and making a few associations. But the demands of life soon intervened, and I forgot all about it. It had not been transcribed into any of my dream notebooks.

The *chance re-appearance* of this strange phrase in the midst of my Caborca writing and my preparations for the return trip, was uncanny. Again, it was like finding a key, but to an unknown lock. I tackled the bizarre images with renewed interest.

I associated the image of the "Fool for Christ" with Saint Francis, who was known as "God's Fool." In becoming God's Fool, Francis also became a fool to his fellows, sacrificing ego pride, risking ridicule, contempt and incomprehension, in order to follow God's will without hesitation, in flagrant disregard for the established canons of the Church as mediator of the Divine. Francis took off his clothes in the streets and renounced his wealthy, cloth-merchant father. Today, of course, we would arrest him for indecency and lock him up as a madman. But there are many kinds of madness, and something in me wants to look gently upon the ecstasies of mystics like Francis, Teresa, Meister Eckhart, etc., troublesome though they might be for the Church and for society.

166

In the end, the sly genius of Catholic tradition elevated his madness and foolishness to a saintly rank. By canonizing and idealizing Francis, the Church was able to protect herself and her followers from the raw, infectious, foolish madness of her visionary son, while capitalizing on his popularity. At the same time the image of Francis was preserved, guaranteed and elevated, "Francis" now a *saint*, an eternal figure who never dies, an image of the potential for divine madness, ecstasy and love inherent in all of us. And if we keep in mind Jung's demonstrations of the parallels between the Christ-image and archetypal individuation symbolism, we can see the "Fool for Christ" psychologically, as an image of what I like to think of as "the Franciscan way of individuation," a particular avenue of individual relationship to the totality of the Self. As an individuation symbol, "Francis" shows the possibility of a totalization of the love of God. It is this Love of God, this *Amor de Dios*, which the voice or presence in the scribbled statement seemed to personify, as if an angel were announcing the inherent possibility of divine love. The same *Amor de Dios*, in my opinion, is what enabled Francis to commune with the birds and animals, hence the many bronze sculptures and the paintings of him with birds on his hands and shoulders, perhaps a donkey at his side.

And the "Paraclete of Caborca?"

What strangeness inheres in this image! Earlier I quoted Jung: "But the eternal promise for him who bears his own cross is the Paraclete." The original Greek term for Paraclete, *parakletos*, derives from *para*, *"beside,"* and *kalein*, *"to call,"* in the sense of "advocate," "comforter," or "one who is called to the side of." In post-Greek Christian usage, it refers to the intervention of the Holy Spirit in human life. In Christian theology, it is in the form of the Paraclete that Christ, after his death and ascension to heaven, will return to *dwell* among humans. But since the Paraclete is supposed to be an "indwelling" Holy Spirit, I take it as a symbolic reference to something *inherent*, some transpersonal factor *embedded* in the human personality, a *universal potential* in each individual—Christian or not. Like an instinct. Like an archetype. Think of it as a felt experience of the spirit of the whole, or, as Jung called the Paraclete, "the Spirit of Truth and Wholeness."

Psychologically, this corresponds to the quality of experience attaching to those moments in which our normal ego-state of fragmentation and division is overcome, and we experience both ourselves and the world from a more complete perspective. I think of it as *epiphanic*. It gives one the felt sense that there is an organizing agent binding together otherwise disparate events, fusing them into a meaningful whole.

I have had several epiphanies in my life, from early childhood onward. They cannot be willed or faked. They are autonomous. And they are *creatively* "wrought" as well, hence they surprise us with their uniqueness. But they do share a few commonalities. Jung's writings are full of references to these kinds of *numinous* experiences, which to me are part and parcel of the phenomenology of *synchronicity*. Curiously, I just now happened to open my volume of *Cosmos and Psyche,* by Richard Tarnas, to a page where he summarizes Jung's many references to the numinous and the synchronistic. Here are Tarnas's words:

> Jung repeatedly described the appearance of the numinous as the abrupt intrusion of another reality into the ordinary conscious state, as something that suddenly crosses one's path, that stops one up short, that is imbued with an uncanny, challenging, often destabilizing quality. It overwhelms one with its alterity. It is autonomous, tricksterlike, beyond anticipation or control.
>
> Such an understanding and experience can be seen as underlying Jung's entire psychology with its distinctive emphasis on the unpredictable, autonomous and ultimately spiritual nature of the unconscious in its interaction with the conscious ego. Through this lens Jung saw the nature and function of dreams, psychological symptoms, slips and

errors, synchronicities, suddenly intrusive
events whether inner or outer, "fate"—the
entire modus operandi of the archetypal
dimension as it unpredictably impressed itself
upon human experience. The very
phenomenon of synchronicity can be
recognized as a vivid expression of precisely
these two archetypal principles in close
interplay: the metaphysical trickster, the
unexpected correspondence of inner and outer
events that reveals a deeper coherence of
meaning in life than had been assumed
possible, the inexplicable coincidence that
carries a numinous charge, the sudden
revelation of a spiritual purpose that works
within and subverts the apparent randomness
of existence.[28]

This brief excerpt summarizing Jung's extensive writings,
goes to the heart of my experiences since the sudden
irruption of fate into my life at Caborca, in the Mexico of 1963.
In a slightly different context, Jung said: "Every encounter with
the Self is a defeat for the ego." I have experienced the truth
of that statement as well. In fact, the entire account of my
experiences in and around Caborca, bears witness to that
truth. But Jung's references to the Paraclete point to another
experience of the Self—after the defeat, a gift.

After crisis, an enlargement and deepening of the spirit, a
consequence of bearing the variegated burden of one's
totality, one's "cross." An "eternal promise," which suggests
the experience is open to anyone who can stand up
consciously to the tension of inner conflicts, no small task. If
we take "eternal promise" not as a metaphysical concretism
but as a statement about the psyche, it suggests that the
Paraclete is something we carry within, that "comes to our
assistance" and bestows upon us the strength and courage
necessary to endure the storms and trials of life and death
with equanimity. An awareness of the presence of this force
can strengthen and comfort the soul open to it. Taken as a

given potential within each of us, then, it is an attitude toward life whose origin and whose boundaries—if it has any boundaries—certainly transcend those of the ego. Its effect is to connect us to the larger life of which our consciousness constitutes but a small yet precious portion.

Had a human speaker—a person on the street—approached me saying seriously, "I am the Fool for Christ and the Paraclete of Caborca," I would have wondered if that person was nuts—that is, *identified with an archetype,* which can sometimes lead to madness. It would be like saying, in all literal naïveté, "I am Napoleon" or "I am Julius Caesar" or "I am Jesus Christ." A grandiose inflation, *if taken literally,* and rich material for psychiatrists and humorists.

However, in my re-discovered, scribbled notation there was no hint of a subjective, rational, empirical person speaking, despite the use of the first-person-singular pronoun standing in for an unknown "I." And since the statement had the character of a dream, I decided not to dismiss it but to treat it symbolically, as if it *were* a dream-statement. Seen in that light, the message took on a decidedly *transpersonal* character, as if it were not so much a madman speaking, but more like the archetype with which the madman identifies, taking on a voice.

I may be stretching the limits of the reader's credulity with this next idea—though I am not asking anyone to "believe" anything—but I can even imagine that the Caborca referred to in the strange quotation actually, in some paranormal way, also refers to "my Caborca." I know that sounds crazy too, like a psychiatrist's diagnostic category of "ideas of reference." But the synchronicities and relativities of the archetypal psyche are capable of such "impossibilities." Jung took great care to lay out the premises underlying his hypothesis of *synchronicity.*

This ambiguity between the utterances of the insane and the utterances of the gods, is a typical problem in the experience of what we might call *the relations between the personal and transpersonal aspects of the psyche, between ego and archetype.* It is the problem of the interactions between the human and the divine realms, ego and Other, the sacred and the profane, familiar ground to poets and mystics, evangelists and schizophrenics, oracles and children, prophets and seers. Jung himself observed many similarities between the spontaneous images he encountered during his "confrontation with the unconscious" and the delusions of the insane. As Jung observes in his autobiography:

> It is of course ironical that I, a psychiatrist, should at almost every step of my experiment have run into the same psychic material which is the stuff of psychosis and is found in the insane. This is the fund of unconscious images which fatally confuse the mental patient. But it is also the matrix of a mythopoeic imagination which has vanished from our rational age. Though such imagination is present everywhere, it is both tabooed and dreaded, so that it even appears to be a risky experiment or a questionable adventure to entrust oneself to the uncertain path that leads into the depths of the unconscious. It is considered the path of error, of equivocation and misunderstanding . . . Unpopular, ambiguous and dangerous, it is a voyage of discovery to the other pole of the world.[29]

Unconscious imagery can indeed be dangerous, thanks to its potency, elusiveness and ambiguity. As Jung points out, it can "fatally confuse" the individual to whom it appears. Perhaps this has been true throughout history and may explain in part why primitive cultures require such elaborate precautions, rituals and taboos, in order to protect themselves from the gods or the spirit-world, i.e., from the powers of the unconscious. In archaic times, however, "protection from" the spirit-world often meant, as well, something like "cordial and ritual relations with" the spirit-world. The rituals were sometimes even specified by the spirits themselves, in the course of induced trances, dreams and spontaneous visions, so there was a degree of formality, we could say, even though the teachings from "elsewhere," being creatively unpredictable, might violate established categories and practices. I would guess that's one reason why monotheistic religions tend to have "jealous" gods and treat shamanic and mystical practices harshly.

Witness, for example, the Christian tradition's efforts to burn out both the pagan influences upon which it was built, as well as any deviation from its authority (the so-called "heresies," often punishable by death). For centuries Christianity has essentially refused the mythopoeic imagination.[30] Instead, our Western tradition has by and large chosen to cultivate doctrinal images over the spontaneous psyche, parable over living symbol, and to base our psychological attitudes more upon collectively-validated truths or doctrines than on the individual's unique experience of interiority—i.e., interactions with "the spirit-world."

Ironically, it is just this same tradition of Christian spiritual attitudes and disciplines that helped establish the foundations of modern science, which latter, through its rigorous methods and exacting logic has carried on the Church's mission of denying the "pagan" imagination in the name of a highly-differentiated, collectively-validated scientific truth. *Catholic* means universal, and today Science has become more catholic than the Church. In stripping ourselves of "superstition" we invoke the rationalism of science to justify our denial of the *spontaneously imagining soul or psyche*, which the Church has been doing for centuries under the banner of cleansing the soul and protecting it from "pagan" influences. Whenever we set up "myth" and "truth" as opposites, we unwittingly deny the mythic wellsprings of creativity we all carry within ourselves.

When I first moved to Puget Sound, I was sampling every unorthodox pathway that opened up to me. One thing I did was go to the waterfront coffee shop every morning and begin conducting my own personal *association experiment*.[31] I picked up a newspaper and, with my eyes closed, I let the tip of my pencil settle on one word at random. With that single word as a starting point, I began writing words down as fast as possible—whatever came to mind, without reservation, like Freud's dictum regarding *free association*. I soon had several pages of three columns each. (This was years before the *heron's beak* writing dream.) The experiment was so interesting that the next morning I did it again. Since I was not trying to control the direction in which things went, let alone the outcome, I ended up—again—with several pages of several columns, only this time the associations had begun to assume two-word combinations. On the third morning I did it again, and, still with no effort to control on my part, the associative word-clusters began coming in threes. I realized that those clusters amounted to what I called at the time, "poetic nuggets," i.e., the germs of poems.

That was the beginning of a madcap rush of writing, all more or less spontaneous. My notebooks filled with dream-texts and with writing. I realized that my perspective on the world was changing. I was beginning to see the world "poetically," as it were, the way a photographer frames images and a fine-art painter sees colors vividly. The further I went along those lines the more I realized that I was making contact with the *mythopoeic layers of the psyche.* I would look at three ravens fighting over spilled french fries on the ground next to a dumpster, but would actually see three church deacons in long, glistening frock coats, formally bowing and praying to one another prior to their service.

Though I have never laid any claim to being a poet, I recognized that my experiences—and the "poetic temperament" and impulses they revealed—were open to any intrepid souls who were willing to expose themselves to their own depths, and from that basis to the depths of the world-soul. The most precious things are not only rare and "difficult to attain," but they are also found in the commonplace. I soon found out that the old alchemists had long ago trod that ground. Jung carved this alchemical maxim on a large stone block that he placed in his garden:

> Here stands the mean, uncomely
> stone, "Tis very cheap in price!
> The more it is despised by fools,
> The more loved by the wise."

173

There are many other versions of this alchemical insight. It basically says that the treasure we seek is right in front of our noses. But we have to learn how to see it first. We must first have "eyes to see," which is probably what makes it so precious. All of the several epiphanies I have experienced in my life, and all of the most powerful synchronicities, have taken place *in this world*, in all its *what-is-ness*. Epiphanies can even occur in dreams, which also *belong to this world—even if they are not entirely contained by this world, and can bring us messages from somewhere else.*³²

The "intervening force" that disrupts my intentions—to which Jung and Tarnas referred—belongs to the cosmos, just as you and I do. As a result of those kinds of epiphanic experiences over the course of my life, I see and experience this world as shot through with sacred, divine, cosmic energies—just as you and I are. Our contingent lives connect us with what may just be non-contingent phenomena.

Some Consequences of Our Legacy

ONE PSYCHOLOGICAL CONSEQUENCE OF OUR BATTERED historical legacy is that, by and large, the *primordial imagination*, our very birthright—as sometimes bodied forth in dreams and hailing back at least to the evolution of *vertebrates* on the planet about 525 million years ago—goes unhonored, unreflected and undifferentiated in our time. This is understandable, to a degree, because to establish a *differentiated relationship to the primordial psyche* is a task which requires a fairly high degree of individual culture, not to mention raw courage. It is not advisable to attempt such an effort from the standpoint of conformity or collectivity, skepticism or nihilism.

Thanks to our *habitual fear and refusal of dreams*, for example, when the primordial psyche does appear it may very well take on what may seem like, or may actually be, a "demonic" form. If we are afraid of our own shadow, we will most likely see frightening images looming out of that shadow. *The horror-movie industry makes a fortune off of our symptomatic fear of the interior realm. Endless war is another profitable symptom of our inner discord.* The horrific images and figures of "enemies" and "threats" keep coming after us, like my childhood dream-gorilla. And rather than get to know them and differentiate them into familiar contents of consciousness—even if it costs us a struggle with *conflicting values*—we keep trying to avoid them and, ultimately, kill them. You can feel the relief in the movie audience when the gruesome image of what threatens the protagonist is finally dead. Once in a rare while, a film manages to capture the creative potential in the alien unconscious and reveal an unexpected, benevolent side to the primordial psyche, on the *other side* of what frightens us.[33] Speaking of fear, Jung once said, in effect, that our greatest fear is the starting point of our greatest growth. Something to think about.

When an entire culture is deficient in one area, most individuals within that culture will share the deficiency. Our culture's refusal of the multivalent imagination renders most of us incapable of meeting it effectively. Consequently, in so many encounters with the living forces of the objective psyche, whether it be through dreams, fantasies, emotions or waking events, the individual ego usually lacks the necessary tools of discrimination—the "sword"—which would permit a creative adaptation to the immense power of these images and the creative forces they depict and embody. The response is too often an appeal to collective solutions. Instead of relating to the dream figure that's pursuing us—finding out its name, for example, or asking what it wants from us—the dreamer calls in the cops, who enforce the collective order at the expense of an individual response to the image.

The cumulative result of this general attitude is an inner impoverishment combined with an often-intense outpouring of violence. When this otherwise individual condition reaches epidemic proportions within a population, some form of disaster is likely to occur. Sooner or later "the shadow" will express itself. In his stirring essay "After the Catastrophe," written in the immediate aftermath of WWII, Jung wrote:

Everything possible has been done for the outside world: science has been refined to an unimaginable extent; technical achievement has reached an almost uncanny degree of perfection. But what of man, who is expected to administer all these blessings in a reasonable way? He has simply been taken for granted. No one has stopped to consider that neither morally nor psychologically is he in any way adapted to such changes. As blithely as any child of nature he sets about enjoying these dangerous playthings, completely oblivious of the shadow lurking behind him, ready to seize them in its greedy grasp and turn them against a still infantile and unconscious humanity.[34]

The social and environmental costs of this general lack of inner discernment and psychological culture are staggering. We subject ourselves and one another—not to mention our fellow creatures, the animals—to great torment simply because we cannot adequately differentiate our inner lives. Collectively speaking, then, we are for the most part strangers to ourselves and afraid of our own shadows. Fortunately, we still have Jung's massive and pioneering work available to us as a psychological foundation on which we may yet learn to build. There may come a time in which new and deeper structures of consciousness will compensate this historical imbalance we have all inherited. There may come a time in which significant numbers of us learn to accept and differentiate our own inner darkness, healing our inner divisions and recovering in the process the discarded values of the soul.

A Movie Madman

SEVERAL WEEKS AFTER I HAD RETURNED FROM CABORCA and my mother's funeral, I spoke with a friend about some of my experiences. When I mentioned the image of the "Fool for Christ and the Paraclete of Caborca," he sat up and told me he had heard the phrase before. "What? Where?" I asked. He thought a moment and recalled many years earlier having seen an old George C. Scott movie (*The Hospital,* 1971)[35] in which a madman was running around a hospital shouting "I am the Fool for Christ and the Paraclete of Caborca." That's all he could remember. Naturally I was stunned, since I had assumed those very phrases belonged to a dream of mine. How could my friend have possibly heard them?

Sometime after that conversation I acquired a copy of the screenplay, written by Paddy Chayefsky, and finally got the entire quote, as written: "I am the Fool for Christ and the Paraclete of Caborca, the Wrath of the Lamb and the Angel of the Bottomless Pit." I had to accept the fact that these images, which by now were quite important to me, had not come from a dream after all, but were the psychotic utterances of a *fictional madman.* Reverend Drummond was running around a hospital dressed as a doctor, arranging the deaths of people "the Lord" had singled out to him as needing to be "taken to his bosom." Before being discovered, he had killed two doctors and a nurse, by arranging for them to become patients, swapping medical charts and medications, and so forth. At one point he even tried to strangle George C. Scott with a stethoscope tube. The fact that Drummond, in his psychotic state, thought he was acting out of a sense of vocation, that he felt he was an instrument of the Lord and had a calling to carry out "God's will," naturally made me a little uncomfortable. Wasn't that more or less what I was doing by returning to Caborca? By writing this book?

Was I not also giving myself over to the dictates of something larger than myself? Well, yes, I was, but . . . This irony, however, did not dampen my enthusiasm for the images of the Fool for Christ and the Paraclete of Caborca, but it did show up the reality of the Christian shadow, the dark side of our religious tradition with its callings and crusades, its servants and soldiers for Christ, its ministries, missions and missionaries. The history of Christian civilization has a dark

177

side indeed, and the blood that stains the Cross is not that of Jesus alone. There is a dark crusader in each of us—Christian or not—ready to impose the "will of God" upon our heathen neighbor, "for his own good." It doesn't even require a madman.

I accepted the chastening message from this strange movie, once again acknowledging the Christian crusader in my own shadow, as well as my own potential for madness were I to fall into a blind identification with the archetypes. Nevertheless I stood firm with my sense of the significance and validity of these two "crazy" images—the Fool for Christ and the Paraclete of Caborca—with my conviction that a larger truth than my own informs both the events of my experiences and the arcane testimony of this book growing out of them.

In the end, the reality of the shadow, including its marbled veins of madness, adds as much to the experience of life as do the "truths" of the ego, which can and do change, though they be of a different valence. In fact, how can we possibly approximate or realize wholeness of being if we do not acknowledge and somehow learn to *integrate our shadows into consciousness*, to some extent at least? If we do not undergo the *often severe conflict of values* that a confrontation with the shadow inevitably entails, then the inner conflicts of individuals are likely to be acted out in the world.

As for the strange quote, the very fact that it popped up when it did—while planning for my dreaded return trip to Caborca—gave it the challenging validity of *synchronistic timeliness*: A scrap of paper several years old, lost in a pile of odds and ends beside my desk, floats to the surface just when I need an orienting image. How timely! The more I continue to work on the quote as a symbolic image, the more value it yields. In the end I can even appreciate the irony of its source in a movie, if only because I finally trust myself to discern between demons and angels, because I have learned the difference between wounding images that are "only crazy" and healing images that reveal the background workings of an objective, transpersonal truth. Jung speaks eloquently of this experience:

> Only the living presence of the divine images
> can lend the human psyche a dignity which
> makes it morally possible for a man to stand
> with himself. Only then will he realize that the
> conflict is in him, that the discord and
> tribulation are his riches, which should not be
> squandered by attacking others; and that, if
> fate should exact a debt from him in the form
> of guilt, it is a debt to himself. (CW 14:511)

The bizarre image—"I am the Fool for Christ and the Paraclete of Caborca"—brought me face to face yet again with the darkness of the shadow, but it also presented me with an image of divine radiance and healing wisdom. It gave me a deepening sense of the mysterious workings of destiny and of the transcendent aspects of the Self. It is a reminder to me and to others that the *call to vocation* is indeed a double-edged sword, cutting this way as well as that. It reminds us that, in the end, there is a fine line between saving a soul and mutilating it, between mass salvation and cultural genocide, between white magic and black and, ultimately, between truth and falsehood.

PART NINE
The Will of God

The decisive question for man is: Is he related to something infinite or not? That is the telling question of his life. Only if we know that the thing which truly matters is the infinite can we avoid fixing our interests upon futilities, and upon all kinds of goals which are not of real importance.[36]

—C. G. Jung

THE WORK I DID ON MY EARLY CHILDHOOD MEMORIES, before beginning to write about Caborca, led me to the conclusion that I had *always* been inclined toward the mysterious, toward surprising incursions of the *numinous* into my life. For me, the earliest such encounters I remembered often took the form of fascination with animals, with trees and blossoms and other forms of life, or explorations of strange places.

As I wrote and delved, many memories from between the ages of two and three piled up: At age two I discovered a ground-squirrel that lived in the drain-pipe of a retaining wall, and hid his *cache* of edible nuts and seeds there. I witnessed and fell in love with a honeybee busily gathering pollen from a brilliant, fuchsia-colored ice plant blossom in bright sunlight—their combined *beauty* overwhelmed me. I once accompanied my mother and grandmother on a visit to a famous cemetery, where I saw a life-sized marble sculpture of Adam and Eve standing on a tall marble pedestal. Looking up at Adam, I was surprised by the marble fig leaf that covered his private parts. When I asked my mother why the fig leaf was there, she explained about the Garden of Eden and how Adam and Eve

181

were ashamed when they realized they were naked, hence the fig leaf. When we got home, I realized that we too had a fig tree in our back yard. With Adam and Eve still on my mind, I plucked a large fig leaf and stuck the stem between my little legs and held it there, covering *my* private parts—though I was clothed—wondering if *I* should feel ashamed as well, still wondering why. At the bottom of the steep hill where we lived at the time, there was a storm drain under the sidewalk. I found I could slither through the slot-shaped opening under the curb, and into a small concrete plenum of sorts, where larger volumes of water could gather. From there I could slide down an underground concrete spillway, walk across the large main drainage-tunnel running parallel to and beneath the street, and cross over to the other side where another, taller spillway fed down into the system. I couldn't climb out of that side by myself—the spillway was too high and slippery, and I was too small. I had to cross back to the other side and slither up and out again through the slot under the sidewalk. While exploring in the back yard one day I crawled behind a majestic clump of pampas grass with feathery plumes on top, and found, on the other side of a wire fence, a neighbor's tiny concrete pond with algae growing in it and two or three brilliant goldfish drifting sluggishly in the green water. As with the honeybee and fuchsia ice plant blossom, the colors alone, plus the hidden seclusion of the little pond and the secret life it contained, fascinated me. I knew that the skimpy fence marked some kind of boundary I was not supposed to cross, but the lure of the tiny green pond and its brilliant little fish were too much to resist. I didn't do anything to disturb or harm the fish or the neighbor. I just stared in fascination at the Edenic scene. As with Adam and Eve eating the forbidden fruit of the Tree of Knowledge, some prohibitions are meant to be violated.

At age five, I heard a mockingbird one afternoon as it sat in a eucalyptus tree in front of our house, singing its heart out, improvising for ten or fifteen minutes while I listened in rapture, my first experience of a mockingbird in full song. What virtuosity! Since my family's culture was centered around church, that mockingbird might have provided my first experience of real music beyond the church organ and the uninspiring hymns. At the same age, while my neighbors were on vacation, I was assigned the duty of collecting eggs every morning from the henhouse in their backyard. When I entered the shed and reached underneath the sitting hens, taking the warm eggs and placing them in a basket, I noticed that one hen was in the process of laying an egg. I was amazed to see what I later learned was an *ovipositor,* a sort of glistening, reddish tube that looked like someone's inverted cheeks or a protruding tongue they had curled up. No one had ever told me about this phenomenon, so it had the impact of something primordial, forbidden. A secret. I never told anyone about seeing it. But I instantly recalled that event decades later in Puget Sound, when I heard Dylan Thomas reading his poems and stories on an LP record. In his marvelous poet's voice he recited these words from "Quite Early One Morning," describing what I took to be a rather unpleasant man, a type of shallow, pretentious poet, very thin, but *"with lips as fulsome, sensual and inviting as a hen's ovipositor."*

At age six, walking home from school one hot afternoon, I stopped to watch a gardener irrigating an orange grove. From a cylindrical, vertical, concrete standpipe about as tall as I was, with tubes projecting outward from it like jets, cool water gurgled forth, spilling into long feeder canals. From there it magically flowed upward through curved siphon tubes, over the canal-banks and into the smaller channels running between the rows of green trees. The heat of the day, combined with the coolness of the water and the shade of the trees, stopped my progress walking home. I was stunned. The gardener watched me with a smile. I think he knew I was having "an experience." I hadn't yet noticed that all the orange trees were covered with blossoms. Then suddenly I was enveloped by the heavenly fragrance of the entire grove, lofted in my direction on a puff of breeze. My first thought was of the Sunday School images of heaven as a place where "the streets are paved with gold, running with milk and honey." Then I realized that was the wrong image. That wasn't it at all. *This* was it. And to this day I still remember saying to myself, at age six: "So *this* is what heaven is like!"

At age nine, I saw black polliwogs turning into tiny frogs in a storm-runoff catch-basin in the hills, the mysterious transformations taking place in a matter of days. Prior to the great event, I took some polliwogs home in a discarded tin can, filled a tub with water and poured them into it. They seemed to accept their new environment, wiggling around happily, or so it seemed to me. A few days later I looked in the tub and discovered they were gone. Where were they? Then I looked at the grass and all the polliwogs, now baby frogs, were hopping around the yard, finding suitable new homes, I hoped. Back at the catch-basin, the remaining polliwogs were also gone. Little frogs hopped in every direction. I didn't really know anything about biology, but I knew a transformation had taken place. Black polliwogs with tails = green frogs with legs. Incredible.

At age eleven or twelve, while exploring the labyrinth of the orange grove behind our house, I came upon a secluded clearing among the green trees. It was a different grove, in a different town, in a different county. As I walked further into the unexpected clearing, I noticed some parted stalks of tall, dry grass. I approached slowly and with interest, but was startled by a sudden, breathtaking flash of blurred auburn wings as a pheasant burst up in alarm from its hidden nest among the yellow-green grasses of the clearing. My heart leaped with the bird. I remember being flushed with—I didn't know what. Love? Desire? Lust? A feeling of warmth crept over my body, suffusing my cheeks. A pheasant flew from the grass, and I learned more about God in that single auburn flash than I had in a hundred Sunday sermons.

I kneeled down before the nest and saw three priceless blue eggs, three unbroken promises waiting to come true, three living prophecies of bounty and abundance to come. *I really wanted to take those eggs*—just as the diver wants to take the pearl, the archeologist the crown, the champion the prize, the sparrow hawk the sparrow, the jeweler the diamond, as the sun takes the moon, the tide takes the pool and the bull takes the soft and irresistible cow.

After a moment I stood up. I hovered at the foot of the nest, then turned and left. As I walked back through the trees, I committed to memory the green-leafed coordinates that would lead me back to the jeweled nest. I knew I would return.

I did not take the eggs.

For two consecutive days I returned to that clearing every afternoon, to make sure the eggs were still there, that the chicks inside hadn't given up hope. On the third day, after school, I went to the grove to check the nest and the eggs.

But the orange grove was gone: trunk, root, branch, leaf, blossom, and crown. The trees had been bulldozed into piles and were being set on fire. My heart broke with the eggs. I was racked with choking disbelief. I stumbled through the debris, gasping and sobbing: What have they done? What are they doing? What about the pheasant? What about the nest? What about the eggs? What about the trees?

I mark that event as the end of my childhood. And I have often wondered, with the exponential increases in human population and the resulting exponential losses of animal habitats, how many other children—let alone pheasants— have had similar experiences to mine. Sometimes I think all humans, our entire species—whether we know it or not—all suffer from deep forms of environmental PTSD and primordial guilt, barely pasted over with the gilding of our technological accomplishments—but at what cost?

Was I a child mystic? Probably. Did I abandon those mystical pursuits when I entered the treacherous shoals of puberty? Increasingly, yes. I was certainly witness to a post-WW2 demographic explosion in Southern California, which triggered a widespread blitz-krieg of destruction in the name of "progress"— orange groves, walnut groves, lemon groves, and many kinds of other trees, and practically every animal habitat short of metropolitan pigeons, cockroaches and spiders, perhaps, falling in every direction by the day. Starting in 1955, the town where I went to high school "grew" in ten years from 5000 to 150,000 inhabitants. What should we call that rate of population increase? I think the reason the number did not increase *ad infinitum* was simply because it had been *built out* to the maximum. There was no room left for building, only demolition and re-building, in a sort of architectural palimpsest—re-writing the material scriptures of modernity.

I did not abandon altogether my secret "mystical pursuits"—the pheasant, the groves, the ravens and doves—and the arcane observations and sensitivities that accompanied them, though I never knew enough to recognize them as such. But practically and outwardly speaking? Yes, I did abandon the best parts of my secret, mystical life.

It's a miracle I didn't seek refuge in some bizarre form of juvenile delinquency, since my child's life to that point had been repeatedly fractured by frequent moves, often during the school year, and I think I was embittered by the loss of so much beauty and by the *intentionally constructed ugliness* that replaced it, everywhere I looked. "Who are the so-called architects that get paid for designing this ugly crap?" I often wondered, as it gradually dawned on me just what a hideous wasteland was being constructed where once so much beauty had stood.

I was being naïve, of course.

Years later, I confessed my feelings to my mother about the destroyed orange groves—"our grove" in particular, *the pheasant's grove*. Her response startled me: "But they paid earnest money!" She was only speaking from the dominant viewpoint, I know. She didn't seem to have a clue as to why I should have such bitter feelings about the juggernaut of "development" in post-war America, and I had no way of explaining to her why I felt the way I did. I barely knew myself, back then. But I was also guilty of the crime, since my first summer jobs were working as a laborer on *construction projects*!

As if in compensation—it was the year of the pheasant and the loss of the grove—my parents stopped moving and we lived in the *same house* throughout my high school years. With that astonishing period of relative stability, my grades shot up, I discovered that I was good at sports, good at foreign languages, and suddenly I turned my attention outward—to grades, track medals and plastic trophies, and, above all . . . *popularity*, one of those shallow pursuits Jung mentioned above.

I see now how difficult it is to maintain an off-beat, introverted, personality orientation—especially a mystical one—when the stilted demands of superficial teenage society in high school and college press their pre-emptive, self-conscious, all-consuming claims, while suppressing the natural prerogatives of the deeper soul. Popularity concerns, then, or their obverse—the horrors of exclusion—for a teenager, often become inflated and inflating preoccupations and mandates. More than a few teenagers actually conceive of suicide as a solution to their problems, a viable "way out."

For myself, as I pledged allegiance to the flag of the *shallow goals of adolescence*, emotional pressures were building inside of me for the release of a deeper, more authentic version of myself—the kernel of which was the mystic child that I had begun to suppress. The more superficially oriented I became, and the more I succeeded at it, the greater the inner pressure became. But what would be the occasion for a release of that pressure? I didn't even know it was coming.

Looking back, I can see a series of mishaps—minor injuries—prior to Caborca, that, in my superficiality and naïveté, I disregarded. I had no idea that those mishaps were *symptoms*, and therefore hints, that *something inside of myself*—broadly speaking, my very interiority itself—needed my serious attention. Until, that is, the force that was making its claim on me from within had built up so much pressure that it finally took over the reins of my life and engineered the "accident" called *Caborca*.

It has taken me *half a century* to figure all this out, and I am still working on it. This is why I was so enthralled with Dylan Thomas's poetry when I arrived at Puget Sound in 1972 and entered the labyrinths of interconnected waterways hosting the herons, with their mysterious habits and haunts, their superb talents.

This poem by Dylan Thomas spoke to me of religious feeling like no preacher in any church ever did.

Maybe the reader is familiar with it:

The force that through the green fuse drives the
flower Drives my green age; that blasts the roots
of trees
Is my destroyer.
And I am dumb to tell the crooked rose
My youth is bent by the same wintry fever.

The force that drives the water through the rocks
Drives my red blood; that dries the mouthing
streams Turns mine to wax.
And I am dumb to mouth unto my veins
How at the mountain stream the same mouth
sucks.

The hand that whirls the water in the pool
Stirs the quicksand; that ropes the blowing wind
Hauls my shroud sail.
And I am dumb to tell the hanging man
How of my clay is made the hangman's lime.

The lips of time leech to the fountain head;
Love drips and gathers, but the fallen blood
Shall calm her sores.
And I am dumb to tell a weather's wind
How time has ticked a heaven round the stars.

And I am dumb to tell the lover's tomb
How at my sheet goes the same crooked worm.

Looking Back

AS I LOOK BACK ON MY CHILDHOOD, I NOW THINK IT MUST have been an innate religious instinct, or something along those lines, that was driving me since my earliest days. But I grew up in a culture which assumed that all forms of divinity were *only to be found in church*, in readings from the Holy Bible, in the sermons and hymns, organs and choirs. As a child I listened intently to the preachers in those churches, but none of them ever spoke to me in my language, the way the mockingbird did, or the pheasant, or the herons—my God, the herons! Or the ravens, doves, owls, nighthawks, coyotes, finches, bushtits and towhees that I listen to now, or the sunrises, moonsets, clouds and trees that I keep watch over today.

Aridity prevails in the high deserts of northern New Mexico where I now live. But rain-clouds and snow-clouds do periodically gather on Ortiz Mountain, from whose peak they sweep across Goldmine Road and down into the Galisteo Basin, where they slide over the uplifted, eroded sandstone outcroppings known as "The Garden of the Gods"—stone deposits from an ancient shallow seabed. Sometimes the clouds, loaded with precious moisture, reach as far as my window while I watch, sometimes not. Other times they come in a flash, with sudden bolts of lightning and peals of thunder, belching out golf-ball-sized hailstones or violent pelting raindrops while I jump and run around the house making sure all the windows are closed, hoping the roof withstands the conflagration.

The "Mexican monsoons" that I knew so little about in 1963, sweltering in Mazatlán with Phil, will sometimes drop three inches of rain here in an hour, pushed by 50-mph winds into horizontal assaults against every fissure in the human-made structures. Under such conditions, it pays to make sure the windows are latched. It also pays not to overestimate the cleverness of *homo sapiens*.

We assign personal names to hurricanes and typhoons, so as to differentiate them, one from another. After all, we wouldn't want to confuse Katrina with Sandy, or Ivan with María. And like weather—mild or violent—we humans also have our own personalities. And like plants and animals, we open or close ourselves according to conditions, preferences and experiences, as the case may be—based on patterns that are repeated through the centuries and millennia. A sage once quipped: "History does not repeat itself, but humans do."

I know it may seem odd, in the light of the "external" conditions I just evoked above, but *if we really want to know ourselves*, we must also find our own way, not only through our responses to the landscapes we inhabit and travel through, or the weather we must either enjoy or endure, but we also must find our way through the dark interiorities of our contemporary experience, in order to locate the specific patterns that resonate with our souls. It has been my experience that the *resonant patterns* most worth seeking are probably—and most thoroughly—revealed in our *dreams*, over time, starting with childhood dreams, if possible. Virtually anyone can do this, if only they will.

In Truth

SINCE THE LOSS OF MY EYE IN 1963, EXPERIENCE HAS amply confirmed the sense that *something else* is governing the *pattern of events* called "Caborca"—something besides accidental meaninglessness. The pattern itself has come to symbolize some essential, perhaps even central, portion of my fate. There is indeed a transpersonal Spirit of Truth and Wholeness, a "Paraclete of Caborca," moving through my life and through the world, organizing and arranging events, and deepening my experience of those events, until I am forced to kneel, as it were, as if before some great power or mystery. To follow the dictates of such a power, insofar as one can discern its promptings, is what I called earlier the "Franciscan way of individuation," the way of divine love, madness and foolishness.

When I think of the Paraclete of Caborca today, I see a great bird—perhaps the heron-man, or an angel, even a *zopilote*—soaring over a desert where human and divine trajectories intersect in collisions of destiny. I see an amazing network of dreams and images, meaningful events, stunning coincidences, impulses and desires—spread over years—in which an *unseen hand* has periodically revealed its presence by *arranging events in the world* in ways that coincided meaningfully with my inner life. I see an entire phase of my development that began symbolically with the loss of an eye and led me through an underground maze of experiences to a vision of the light that glimmers in and behind the dark shapes of the soul. And when I emerge from the dark tunnels into the radiance of this world, and consider our faithful celestial exemplars—the sun and the moon—spinning and orbiting, rising and setting, like hundreds of billions of others, I see the fellowship of the entire *cosmos*, a Greek term for "an ordered arrangement," as for example, "the universe as an embodiment of order, harmony and beauty."

We, The Dominioneers

FOR MILLENNIA, WE HUMANS HAVE PRIDED OURSELVES AS BEING the *presumptive dominioneers* of this planet, but perhaps we did so unwisely. Thomas Berry, in his book *The Dream of the Earth*,[37] thought so, and he summed up our situation with exquisite insight and depth. His words are worth quoting here at length:

> St. John tells us that in the beginning all things took on their shape through the word.[38] The word was seen as psychic and personal. This was the numinous reality through which all things were made and without which was made nothing that has been made. The word, the self-spoken word, by its own spontaneities brought forth the universe and value. This is in accord with Lao Tsu, the Chinese sage, who tells us that the human models itself on the earth, earth models itself on heaven, heaven models itself on tao, tao models itself on its own spontaneity.

This spontaneity as the guiding force of the universe can be thought of as the mysterious impulse whereby the primordial fireball flared forth in its enormous energy, a fireball that was the present in its primordial form, as the present is the fireball in its explicated form. What enabled the formless energies to emerge into such a fantastic variety of expression in shape, color, scent, feeling, thought, and imagination?

As with any aesthetic work, we attribute it especially to the imaginative capacities of the artist, for only out of imaginative power does any grand creative work take shape. Since imagination functions most freely in dream vision, we tend to associate creativity also with dream experience. The dream comes about precisely through the uninhibited spontaneities of which we are speaking. In this context we might say: *In the beginning was the dream.* Through the dream all things were made, and without the dream nothing was made that has been made.

While all things share in this dream, as humans we share in this dream in a special manner. This is the entrancement, the magic of the world about us, its mystery, its ineffable quality. What primordial source could, with no model for guidance, imagine such a fantastic world as that in which we live— the shape of the orchid, the coloring of the fish in the sea, the winds and the rain, the variety of sounds that flow over the earth, the resonant croaking of the bullfrogs, the songs of the crickets, and the pure joy of the predawn singing of the mockingbird?

Experience of such a resplendent world activated the creative imagination of Mozart in The Magic Flute, of Dante in his Divine Comedy, and gave to Shakespeare that range of sensitivity, understanding, and emotion that found expression in his plays. All of these derive from the visionary power that is experienced most profoundly when we are immersed in the depths of our own being and of the cosmic order itself in the dreamworld that unfolds within us in our sleep, or in those visionary moments that seize upon us in our waking hours. There we discover the Platonic forms, the dreams of Brahman, the Hermetic mysteries, the divine ideas of Thomas Aquinas, in infinite worlds of Giordano Bruno, the world soul of the Cambridge Platonists, the self-organizing universe of Ilya Prigogine, the archetypal world of C. G. Jung.

A few pages later Berry continues:

Our secular, rational, industrial society, with its amazing scientific insight and technological skills, has established the first radically anthropocentric society and has thereby broken the primary law of the universe, the law that every component member of the universe should be integral with every other member of the universe and that the primary norm of reality and of value is the universe community itself in its various forms of expression, especially as realized on the planet Earth.

This new industrial coding, which arose first in Western society, has now been spread throughout the entire earth. Few peoples anywhere have escaped its influence. The relation of the human community to its genetic coding and to the entire functioning of the natural world is decisively altered. A profound shift in meaning is given to the entire evolutionary process.

The immediate advantages of this new way of life for its prime beneficiaries have been evident throughout these past two centuries. But, now, suddenly we begin to experience disaster on a scale never before thought possible. For a long while we looked back at prior times and the mythic accounts of how the world came into being, the sequence of transformations and the role of the human in the larger processes of nature; we looked back at these stories, at the revelatory dreams of these earlier peoples, at their sense of numinous energies governing the phenomenal world, at their efforts to establish contact with these powers through strange shamanic performances or through more-programmed initiatory and sacrificial rituals; we looked back at all this with a certain disdain for these dark ages, although with a restrained envy of the visions recorded in their sacred literature, of their heroic experiences, and often of an artistic grandeur that we could not match.

We were the sane, the rational, the dreamless people, the chosen people of destiny. We had found the opening to a more just society, a more reasoning intellectual life. Above all we had the power to re-engineer the planet with our energy systems, our dams and irrigation projects, our great cities. We could clear the forests, drain the marshes, construct our railways and highways, all to the detriment of the other living forms of earth, to the elimination of needed habitat, to the obstruction of migration paths, to the cutting off of access to waterways. We could subdue the wilderness, domesticate the planet. We were finally free from the tyranny of nature. Nature was now our servant, delivering up to us its energies, altering its biological rhythms in accord with our mechanical contrivances.

The human condition could be overcome by entrepreneurial skills. Nuclear energy would give us limitless power. Through genetic engineering we could turn chickens into ever more effective egg-laying machines, cows into milk-making machines, steers into meat-making contrivances, all according to human preference, not according to the inner spontaneities of these living beings as determined by their genetic coding, a coding shaped through some billions of years of experiment and natural selection.

Ever heightened consumption was the way to ultimate human fulfillment. Every earthly being was reduced from its status as a sacred reality to that of being a "natural resource," available for human use for whatever trivial purposes humans might invent. It would take a while to describe what has been happening in all our professions and institutions in this period of assumed cultural progress.

I cannot improve on Thomas Berry's words or his vision. They definitely deserve a careful reading, and re-reading, several times over. His text reminds me of a brief and curious experience I once had. It was like a dream, but I was awake, lying in bed, looking up at the ceiling, my mind drifting. Suddenly I imagined that there was *one single star in the firmament* whose beam was shining directly at me. Of course, the same thing might be said about every star-beam that any of us can see—as if to say, *if we can see it, then it can "see" us, i.e., touch us with its light*. But it seemed to me that the single star I was imagining—perhaps even *feeling*—really was "touching" me with its beam, despite the roof and ceiling over my head.

Of course I know the basics of what is taught, or used to be taught, at various levels in high schools and colleges—that what we call "light" consists of elementary particles, or bundles of electromagnetic energy, in turn called "photons," which travel through what we call "space" at a tremendous, consistent speed, behaving paradoxically like particles or waves. I have no good reason to doubt the findings of generations of scientists in this regard, even if the findings are subject to change.

However, that was not what I *experienced.* The "beam" I *intuitively felt* coming to me from that single star, was more like a *rope* or a *tether,* many trillions of miles long, by means of which the star and I were *attached to one another.* I know this is physically impossible, and it sounds goofy, if not crazy, but that's how it was—a fantasy-image that struck me as being "real," though admittedly quite beyond reason.

We don't have any respectable category for such an experience. I *know* it was a fantasy image, tinged with semi-sensate qualities. Call it a waking dream, if you will, or an unanticipated or hypnagogic vision, or how you might imagine a "message from an angel" to be—like a "ladder to Heaven." Definitely unorthodox, and not ordinary. It occurred about 50 years ago and lasted no more than a minute or so. But as with other such experiences, I haven't forgotten it.

As I think about it now, in the light of Thomas Berry's reflections, the fantasy-image of that "single star" seemed to serve as something like a *badge,* not of honor, but of membership. In other words, the star-experience certified my membership in what Berry calls the "universe community," which I think of as well in terms of a "cosmic fellowship," which includes, needless to say, not only us star-engendered humans,[39] but also the hosts of star-engendered animals with whom we share this beautiful, star-engendered Earth. In short, everything.

In particular, my feeling of fellowship extends at the moment to the exultant choirs of coyotes that sing together at night in the arroyos around my house, to the extent that I would love to thrust my throat skyward and sing with them, one more voice among many, howling out tunes from the coyote hymnal, pumping lungs side by side with my furry brothers and sisters, *mis hermanos y hermanas.*

Or perhaps I might prefer to express my exultation the way my solitary cousin the mockingbird does—*mi primo soltero*— sitting alone on a branch in a eucalyptus tree, or any other tree, singing its heart out, never repeating the melodious notes, the trills and arpeggios—the *falsetas*—of its song. I would gladly take lessons from the mockingbird, that I too might add the improvised uniqueness of my own song to the harmonious hubbub of the grand, cosmic oratorio that started with a big bang, and whose reverberations whisper still in the radiant background of everywhere.

What a fine destiny that would be!

ENDNOTES

1 Tarnas, Richard, *Cosmos and Psyche,* Penguin Group, New York, NY. 2006, p. 403

2 C. G. Jung, CW 11, *Psychology and Religion: West and East,* "A Psychological Approach to the Trinity," par. 265.

3 Jung, C. G., CW 5, *Symbols of Transformation,* reference unknown.

4 Jung, C. G., CW 6, *Psychological Types,* par. 658.

5 Sir James Jeans, *The Mysterious Universe,* 1944, p. 137.

6 Parallax = the perceived change in position of an object seen from two different places. Also, knowing in advance the relative sizes of two objects when side by side—like a car and a pedestrian—I can roughly gauge the distance between them by noting how the relative sizes change with distance and separation. It's a partial compensation for the loss of depth perception. Better than nothing. See https://en.wikipedia.org/wiki/Parallax

7 See my brief essay, "The Flamenco Letra: Architecture of the Emotions" at https://www.academia.edu/35626595/THE_FLAMENCO_LETRA_Architecture_of_the_Emotions

8 See García Lorca's essay, *"Poem of the Deep Song."* https://www.poetryintranslation.com/PITBR/Spanish/DeepSong.php

9 https://www.biblegateway.com/passage/?search=Matthew+20%3A16&version=KJV

10 Jung, C. G., *Psychological Types,* CW 6.

11 Nor did the volumes of Freud that I read in college excite any particular interest in dreams. I found his *theory* too dogmatic, too reductive—though his writing was elegant. In fact, in 1930 Freud was awarded the Goethe Prize for Literature and was nominated several times for the Nobel Prize—in 1936, the Nobel nomination was for *literature.* In 1964, a Sigmund Freud Prize was instituted for excellence in "Scientific Prose."

12 I have come to regard childhood dreams in general—especially chronic ones—as having something to do with one's destiny. Since they are almost invariably archetypal images, because the societal ego-forces have not yet come to dominate the personality, they tend to "hover" over one's later life, yielding value, even when forgotten, or even if they are felt to be "nightmares." How much more value could our childhood dreams yield or release into life, if the dreamer could only carry them in consciousness, recognizing the boon they bring!

13 Jung, C. G., CW 7, *Two Essays on Analytical Psychology*, p. 409

14 https://en.wikipedia.org/wiki/Synchronicity

15 C. G. Jung, CW 9ii, Para 51.

16 *meisterstück* = masterpiece

17 There is a beautiful flamenco *letra* sung by the great singer Camarón de la Isla. It is sung in the *palo* of the *tango gitano:*

Si tus ojitos fueran/Aceitunitas verdes/To'a la noche estaría/Muele que muele/muele que muele/muele que muele. "If your sweet eyes were/little green olives/All night long I would be/Milling and milling/milling and milling/milling and milling."

18 Book of Genesis, 32:22-32

19 Corbin, Henri, *Avicenna and the Visionary Recital* and *Creative Imagination in the Sufism of Ibn Arabi.*

20 For a provocative view of the "philosophical egg" in medieval alchemy, see Jung, C. G., *Psychology and Alchemy,* CW 12, p. 202: "In alchemy the egg stands for the chaos apprehended by the artifex, the prima materia containing the captive world-soul. Out of the egg — symbolized by the round cooking vessel — will rise the eagle or phoenix [Egyptian *bennu bird* or heron], the liberated soul, which is ultimately identical with the Anthropos who was imprisoned in the embrace of Physis."

21 Symbol, from the Greek, *sym,* "together" + *ballein,* "to throw"

22 See Sibudu Cave, South Africa: http://www.uj.ac.za/EN/Newsroom/News/Pages/Stone-Agearrowsfound.aspx

23 Historian of Religion Mircea Eliade, wrote a vast compendium of shamanic practices and traditions entitled *Shamanism: Techniques of Ecstasy*. Taken largely from eye-witness accounts and testimonies from surviving tribal shamans by anthropologists who interviewed them, Eliade's work makes clear the archaic traditions that pre-date the later biblical motifs of spirit-beings, animal-spirits and the conjoined animal-human figures known as angels. See also my essay, "What Is An Angel?" in *The Angels, (The Entities Trilogy),* The Dallas Institute Publications, 1994. Robert Sardello, ed., (p. 63).

24It was reported in the early twentieth-century (Frank G. Speck, 1935, *Naskapi: Hunters of the Labrador Peninsula*) that the *Naskapi* hunting tribes of Labrador, though primitive, had a sophisticated spiritual life in which dreams figured prominently in their culture, particularly in their preparations for the hunt. They would prepare for a hunt by *dreaming* of the location of the game-animals *the night before*. In that way they knew where to go through the primordial forests to find their prey.

25 Jung, C. G., CW 11, *Psychology and Religion, East and West,* par. 379.

26 I admit there was a certain irony in this poem and in the traditional religious associations to "the cross" to which it would be affixed. Those many associations would be misleading if taken literally and applied to me. Even if we shift our glance from the Universal "Catholic" Church, to the current jumble of over 40,000 Protestant denominations (at last count), there are crosses all over the place. Some non-Christians and ex-Christians I have known detest the symbolism of the cross, or the Crucifixion.

Recently I attended a party (rare for me!) and a man I had just met practically exploded when I used the term "religious." I was going to say something about "religious experience," as it pertains to this Caborca book project, but I never got to finish my sentence. "Ah! Religion!" he exclaimed, and with a dismissive gesture brushed the very notion away. He might as well have added, "Bah! Humbug!" It turns out that what I am simply trying to describe herein from my own experiences is apparently subject to explosive emotions.

27 *Cabeza de Vaca,* 16th-century Spanish explorer, shipwreck survivor, captive-slave turned medicine man.
https://en.wikipedia.org/wiki/%C3%81lvar_N%C3%BA%C3%B1ez_Cabeza_de_Vaca

[28] Tarnas, Richard, *Cosmos and Psyche,* p. 403.

[29] Jung, C. G., Jaffé, Aniela, *Memories, Dreams, Reflections*, Vintage Books edition, pp. 188-189.

[30] See James Hillman's "Peaks and Vales" article in *Puer Papers,* Spring Publications, Dallas, TX. 1979.)

[31] Jung invented the "Association Experiment" using the "galvanic skin response," which later formed the basis of the so-called lie-detector test. C. G. Jung, CW2, *Experimental Researches,* 1973, Princeton University Press, Princeton, NJ.

[32] I have often thought of something I call "the Dream Wave." This is a thought-experiment using grade-school arithmetic, applied to the fact that researchers have shown that virtually every person on earth dreams four to five times per night. (We're not counting all mammals, plus other species who also dream.) You can do the math yourself or use a calculator. Multiply, let us say, four (dreams), by the number of people on the planet. Let us say, *seven billion,* even though we are approaching eight billion shortly. Four times seven billion equals roughly twenty-eight billion dreams—in one revolution of the planet. One week yields 196 billion dreams. One month yields 784 billion dreams. One year yields 9 trillion, 408 billion dreams, approximately. You can see that it does not take long to touch on astronomical numbers of dreams on this one planet. What do you come up with? What should we think of this?

[33] Some examples of this are "Jacob's Ladder," "Close Encounters of the Third Kind," and "E.T."

[34] Jung, C. G., CW 10, *Civilization in Transition,* par. 442.

[35] See "The Hospital" screenplay, p. 84.

[36] Jung. C. G., *Memories, Dreams, Reflections,* p. 325.

[37] Berry, Thomas, *The Dream of the Earth,* Sierra Club Books, 1988, pp. 196-198, 202-203.

[38] Notice that Berry does not capitalize "the Word." I suspect he did that for several reasons. One would be to bring the term and its referents closer to modern *experience on earth*, by deflating early Christianity's efforts to theologize (to spirit away from earth) the more worldly ideas of earlier Greek philosophers. The Greeks, pagan though they may have been, were in many ways more *grounded* in their philosophies than the Christians. Also, there may have been a misogynistic element in St. John's

gospel, since the Word and Sophia, or Divine Wisdom, were virtually identical. Sophia was originally known as the *female aspect of God,* i.e., God's Wisdom.

39 I take it for granted as *common knowledge,* that our sun and planets, and all life on earth, ourselves included, originated from the heavy elements compounded in the scarcely imaginable temperatures and pressures generated within exploding stars—super-novae. As one writer phrased it, "the iron that makes your blood red was once inside the heart of an exploding star." If this is not common knowledge, it seems to me that it should be. To say that "we are dreaming stardust," as I sometimes do, is not hyperbole. It is a fact.

PLATES

While writing the last chapters for *The Paraclete of Caborca,* I recently opened a file-folder of old documents, with leftover detritus from the accident in Mexico that occurred over 56 years ago now. I hadn't looked at those documents for quite a while, when I had not gotten so far into telling the story, not to mention the work that editing and finishing a book often entails—deleting, new writing, re-writing, etc. When I held those aging documents in my hand again, I had forgotten about a lot of them.

First was a yellowed envelope bearing the name of a Mexican insurance company, *Seguros Tepeyac.* Phil and I had bought a policy from them before the trip. I shivered at the memory of the name. Inside was a smudged Xerox copy of Phil's Mexican *accident report,* one of the many tasks he had to deal with after I had been flown out of Caborca.

There were also lots of medical invoices and cancelled checks in the folder. After half a century, the prices seemed paltry in comparison to current medical fees but were robust enough at the time. Among them were:

—Receipts from the California hospital, the surgeon and the anesthetist.

—A receipt from a firm of German ocularists who made blown-glass eyes in a tiny green-walled office in downtown LA. I went there not long after the accident and surgery, feeling I was entering a "different world." They had cabinets with flat drawers full of sightless glass eyes that seemed to be peering out. That was creepy, but I needed a cheap, ready-made, temporary glass eye to help the swollen tissues in the socket to subside. I covered the glass eye with a black eye-patch.

—A receipt from the following summer when I began driving to Westwood periodically, where a different prosthetist built up my permanent prosthetic eye out of several layers of cast acrylic. It was a lengthy process requiring many trips, but as I said in the text, he did an excellent job.

—A receipt from the pilot my mother hired to fly me from Tucson to Fullerton airport. Signed by the pilot himself, it was a one-man operation.

There were also a few *photos*, and photocopies, which touched so directly on the story of Caborca and its aftermath, that I began to imagine adding a section of "Plates" to the text. I did not want to "tell the story in pictures," if only because I did not have a complete record. So, I decided to use some of the photos and copies I had, plus any others that would add to the project, to provide *evocations* of the story I had sweated over for so long.

I hope these images will prove "evocative" enough to stimulate the reader's imagination, while helping to round out the book. In that spirit, then, I offer up these Plates, with captions.

PLATE 1

This is the Mexican road sign for Federal Highway 2, which runs south-east from the US border at Sonoyta, Sonora, to Caborca, and from there east to Santa Ana, Sonora, where it meets the junction with Highway 15 running south from the border at Nogales.

PLATE 2

Map of Sonora, México. *NOTE:* Caborca is located about half-way between Santa Ana (directly south of Nogales) and Sonoyta, at the US border near Baja California. Mazatlán is located in the state of Sinaloa, to the south, and does not appear on this map.

PLATE 3

Saguaro cacti in the Great Desert of Sonora, raising their arms
in salute. These giant cacti are characteristic of this desert
ecology, at lower elevations, in both northern Mexico and
southern Arizona. To me, as I see them mythopoetically, they
resemble a standing army of loyal retainers saluting their
leader, the Sun.

PLATE 4

Phil White visiting me at home, about one year *after* the accident
in Caborca, ca. late 1964.

PLATE 5

Caborca Before-and-After photos. Left: Bob's high school graduation photo, 1960. Right: Now known as "Paco," a nickname that stuck and has lasted for over fifty years. This second photo was taken about 8 or 10 years after the accident.

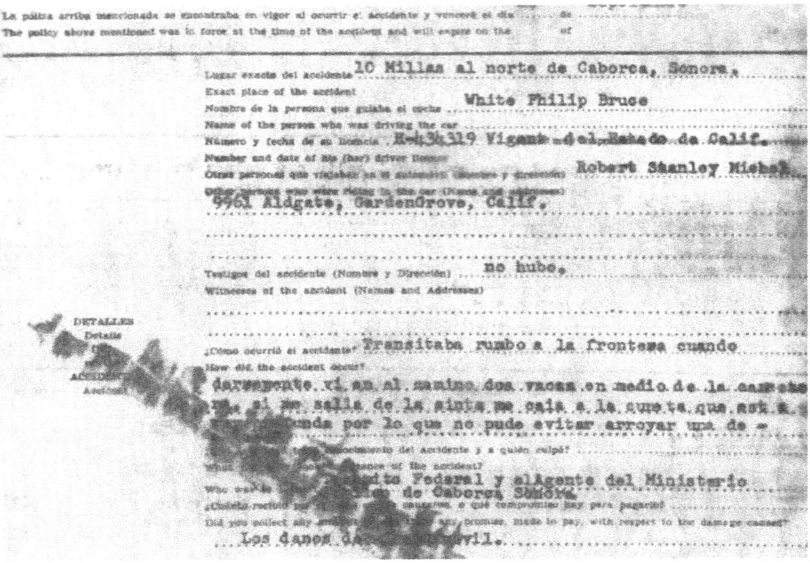
La póliza arriba mencionada se encontraba en vigor al ocurrir el accidente y vencerá el día ...... de
The policy above mentioned was in force at the time of the accident and will expire on the ...... of

Lugar exacto del accidente 10 Millas al norte de Caborca, Sonora.
Exact place of the accident
Nombre de la persona que guiaba el coche White Philip Bruce
Name of the person who was driving the car
Número y fecha de su licencia H-434319 Vigente del Estado de Calif.
Number and date of his (her) driver license
Otras personas que viajaban en el automóvil (Nombre y dirección) Robert Stanley Michel
Other persons who were riding in the car (Name and addresses)
9961 Aldgate, GardenGrove, Calif.

Testigos del accidente (Nombre y Dirección) no hubo.
Witnesses of the accident (Names and Addresses)

DETALLES
Details
ACCIDENTE
Accident

¿Cómo ocurrió el accidente? Transitaba rumbo a la frontera cuando
How did the accident occur?
derepente vi en el camino dos vacas en medio de la carretera
si me salia de la cinta me caia a la cuneta que está
por lo que no pude evitar arroyar una de -
... conocimiento del Accidente y a quién culpó?
... of the accident?
... Federal y el Agente del Ministerio
... de Caborca Sonora.
¿Cobró ... o qué compromiso hay para pagarlo?
Did you collect any ... promise made to pay, with respect to the damage caused?
Los danos ... vil.

PLATE 6

Partial copy of Phil's Mexican auto insurance claim for damages to the VW. The repairs were carried out in Nogales, Sonora.

PLATE 7

Xerox copy of the b/w photograph given to Phil in Caborca in
1963, after the accident. This is the photo I carried with me,
28 years later, on my return trip to Caborca in 1991. I met
three of the men from this photo. They accompanied me into
the desert for the ceremony.

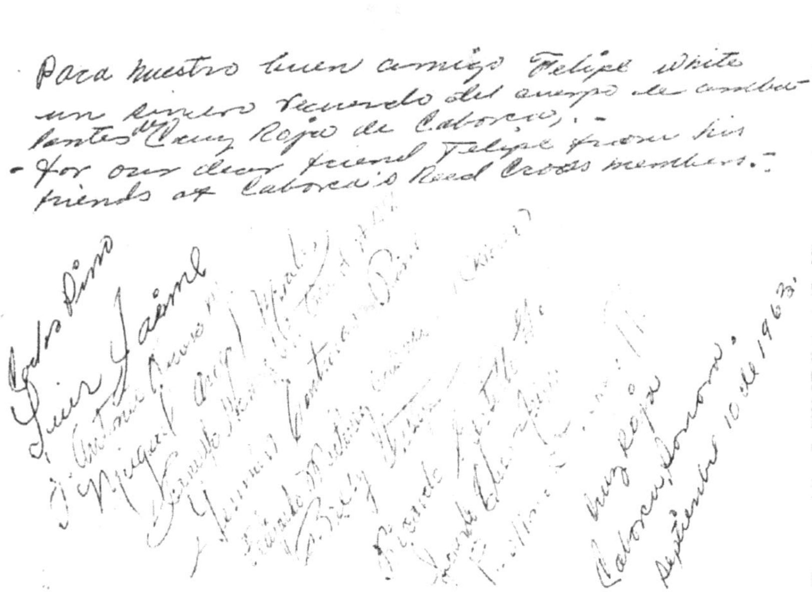

PLATE 8

Back of Red Cross photograph, includes souvenir inscription
above, and signatures of ambulance drivers below. The three
men from this photograph I met on my return trip to Caborca
were: Carlos Pino, Leonardo Jaime Peña and Billy Ortega.

213

PLATE 9

Paco Mitchell playing hand-made Manuel Reyes Spanish flamenco guitar. This photo was taken during the early art-bronze-foundry years in Puget Sound, ca. 1975, hence the white splashes on my right shoulder = plaster from the foundry. A photographer had asked if he could take my photo—as is, no prep needed. So I said, "OK."

PLATE 10

Great Blue Heron in flight, near dusk. This is
similar to what I dimly saw, as it flew away
after dark. That was my first heron encounter, on
the Puget Sound beach at low tide.

PLATE 11

A Great Blue Heron in sunlight, preening its feathers. Notice the
sharpness of the beak. Adult Blue Herons range from 48" to 52" h.
Two of the dream-herons were *six feet tall*.

PLATE 12

Blue Heron Foundry, ca. 1980: A crucible of molten bronze, pouring lost-wax sculpture castings. After firing the molds to red heat in a kiln, to burn out the wax pattern—hence the "lost wax"—the plaster molds are then packed in sand, to reinforce them against ruptures. In addition, bronze ingots are placed on top of the hot empty molds, adding extra weight in case the dense molten metal does break through the bottom of the mold. In that case, without the ingots to weigh it down, the mold will then literally *float* on the pool of molten metal, allowing even more metal to run out the bottom, forming a pool of dense bronze. That would be a "disaster." This crucible, made out of silicon carbide, holds 300 lbs. of bronze. The temperature of the metal at this point in the pour is still close to 2000 degrees F.

PLATE 13

One of Paco's bronze herons, cast at Blue Heron Foundry, ca.
1985. (Ht. ca. 34"-36"). Original model was rendered in clay
over steel armature. Plaster mold taken from model,
duplicated in wax. Cast by "lost-wax" method in five separate

sections, welded together, blue-green patina of copper nitrate with liver of sulfur.

PLATE 14

Egyptian scroll-painting of stylized heron wearing the Atef-crown of Osiris, symbolizing death-and-resurrection. The two feathers on either side are the emblems of Maat, feathers of truth and justice. The painting depicts the mythical *bennu bird* or *phoenix,* a crucial figure in an Egyptian creation myth at *the moment of sunrise* on the First Day. This was the "myth" that I experienced synchronistically after my dream of the two herons on the beach at low tide.

PLATE #15

Paco's linoleum-block print in honor of heron-sunrise dream and
synchronistic event with two herons. Executed ca. late 1980s.

PLATE 16

I set out on my return trip to Caborca on 28 March 1991. This photograph was taken two days later at the "Ceremony of the Cross," 10 mi. west of Caborca, with Red Cross Members attending. (NOTE: The hand-written inscription at the top of the photo is dated 20 April 1992, a year after the ceremony. That's when this photograph was finally sent to me. Manuel González took this photo and was instrumental in the ceremony and many other ways.

PLATE 17

Red Cross Members, *Cruz Roja de Caborca*, back in town, just after the ceremony in the desert. Prof. Manuel González (far right) served as an interpreter and guide; Comandante Gustavo González Grisalva, (front row, with boy). The three members from the 1963 photo who attended the ceremony were: Leonardo Jaime Peña, no hat (back row, left of cross); Billy Ortega, wearing cap (back row, right of cross); Carlos Pino Contreras (yellow windbreaker, red hat).

PLATE 18

I call this, "the ecstatic outpouring of the animal soul." NOTE: The animals do not hold anything back, nor do they pretend to be other than what they are, the way humans do.

PLATE 19

Mockingbird in full song. I first heard a mockingbird singing when I was five or six years old. I was mesmerized. To hear this amazing bird (with doves and traffic in background), go to YouTube link:
https://www.youtube.com/watch?v=PbImHA61P1o

The Paraclete of Caborca: A Collision with Destiny was set in Landa font from Adobe and designed by The Lockhart Press. A complete set of plates, with several in full color, may be seen at:

paraceleteofcaborca.com

The author may be reached at:

mitchell@cybermesa.com

www.ingramcontent.com/pod-product-compliance
Lightning Source LLC
Chambersburg PA
CBHW061012280326
41935CB00009B/937